Lectionary Stories *for* Preaching *and* Teaching

Cycle A

for the Revised Common Lectionary

A Compendium of Stories from
StoryShare
a Component of **SermonSuite.com**
from CSS Publishing Company

CSS Publishing Company, Inc.
Lima, Ohio

LECTIONARY STORIES FOR PREACHING AND TEACHING
CYCLE A

FIRST EDITION
Copyright © 2013
by CSS Publishing Co., Inc.

Published by CSS Publishing Company, Inc., Lima, Ohio 45807. All rights reserved. No part of this publication may be reproduced in any manner whatsoever without the prior permission of the publisher, except in the case of brief quotations embodied in critical articles and reviews. Inquiries should be addressed to: CSS Publishing Company, Inc., Permissions Department, 5450 N. Dixie Highway, Lima, Ohio 45807.

For more information about CSS Publishing Company resources, visit our website at www.csspub.com, email us at csr@csspub.com or call (800) 241-4056.

ISBN-13: 978-0-7880-2704-8
ISBN-10: 0-7880-2704-2   PRINTED IN USA

Table of Contents

Introduction	9
Advent 1 *Matthew 24:36-44* Waiting in the Light	10
Advent 2 *Matthew 3:1-12* Repenting in the Friendly Skies	14
Advent 3 *James 5:7-10* Lessons of a Farmer	18
Advent 4 *Matthew 1:18-25* I'm Pregnant	21
Christmas Eve / Day *Luke 2:1-14* The Great Christmas-Tree Battle	23
Christmas 1 *Matthew 2:13-23* God With Us	26
New Year's Day *Ecclesiates 3:1-13* Christina-Kay's Grandfather	30
Christmas 2 *Ephesians 1:3-14* You Were Adopted	34
Epiphany of Our Lord *Matthew 2:1-12* The Bethlehem Conundrum	36
Baptism of Our Lord / Epiphany 1 / Ordinary Time 1 *Isaiah 42:1-9; Acts 10:34-43* Welcoming Mr. Forsythe	40

Epiphany 2 / Ordinary Time 2   43
John 1:29-42
Too Close for Comfort

Epiphany 3 / Ordinary Time 3   45
Isaiah 9:1-4
One Bright Light

Epiphany 4 / Ordinary Time 4   49
Matthew 5:1-12
Mercy, Mercy

Epiphany 5 / Ordinary Time 5   51
Isaiah 58:1-9a (9b-12)
The Way to God

Epiphany 6 / Ordinary Time 6   54
Deuteronomy 30:15-20
Choose Life

Epiphany 7 / Ordinary Time 7   56
1 Corinthians 3:10-11, 16-23
What Kind of Fool Are You?

Transfiguration of Our Lord   61
(Last Sunday after Epiphany)
Matthew 17:1-9
Jesus Was an Alien!

Ash Wednesday   63
Joel 2:1-2, 12-17
The Terrible Dark Day

Lent 1   66
Genesis 2:15-17; 3:1-7
It's Not My Fault

Lent 2   68
John 3:1-17
Three Field Goals and a Touchdown

Lent 3   72
Romans 5:1-11
The Account

Lent 4   77
John 9:1-41
The Disturbing Witness of Grace

Lent 5   80
Ezekiel 37:1-14
Bones

Passion / Palm Sunday   84
Matthew 26:14—27:66
Is It Truth?

Maundy Thursday   87
1 Corinthians 11:23-26
Do This Remembering Me...

Good Friday   89
Isaiah 52:13—53:12
Reflecting Martyrs

Easter Sunday   93
Acts 10:34-43; Colossians 3:1-4
Anticipation

Easter 2   96
John 20:19-31
Tracks

Easter 3   100
Acts 2:14a, 22-32
Speak the Truth in Love

Easter 4   105
Psalm 23
Familiar Words

Easter 5   107
John 14:1-14
Please Don't Forget Me

Easter 6   110
Acts 17:22-31
Looking for God

Ascension of Our Lord   112
Acts 1:1-11
Wayne's Deployment

Easter 7   115
John 17:1-11
Where's the Finish Line?

Pentecost Sunday   120
1 Corinthians 12:3b-13
A Ducky Miracle

Holy Trinity Sunday   123
2 Corinthians 13:11-13
Benediction

Proper 7 / Pentecost 2 / Ordinary Time 12   125
Romans 6:1b-11
Sin That Grace Abound?

Proper 8 / Pentecost 3 / Ordinary Time 13   128
Matthew 10:40-42
The Tie

Proper 9 / Pentecost 4 / Ordinary Time 14   134
Matthew 11:16-19, 25-30
What Can Brown Do for You?

Proper 10 / Pentecost 5 / Ordinary Time 15   137
Genesis 25:19-34
Taxicab Confessions

Proper 11 / Pentecost 6 / Ordinary Time 16   142
Genesis 28:10-19a
The Land's Sacred

Proper 12 / Pentecost 7 / Ordinary Time 17   145
Romans 8:26-39
Never Again Separate

Proper 13 / Pentecost 8 / Ordinary Time 18   149
Matthew 14:13-21; Psalm 17:1-7, 15
Compassion at Work

Proper 14 / Pentecost 9 / Ordinary Time 19   151
Matthew 14:22-33
Out of the Same Boat With Peter

Proper 15 / Pentecost 10 / Ordinary Time 20   154
Romans 11:1-2a, 29-32
You're Stuck

Proper 16 / Pentecost 11 / Ordinary Time 21   157
Romans 12:1-8
A Rose and a Scarf

Proper 17 / Pentecost 12 / Ordinary Time 22   161
Psalm 105:1-6, 23-26, 45c
A Reason to Tell

Proper 18 / Pentecost 13 / Ordinary Time 23   164
Matthew 18:15-20
Gathered in My Name

Proper 19 / Pentecost 14 / Ordinary Time 24   168
Exodus 14:19-31
The Unsecret Weapon

Proper 20 / Pentecost 15 / Ordinary Time 25   172
Exodus 16:2-15; Philippians 1:21-30
Kristin's Faith

Proper 21 / Pentecost 16 / Ordinary Time 26   175
Matthew 21:23-32
Brokenness to Life

Proper 22 / Pentecost 17 / Ordinary Time 27   179
Psalm 19
qGenesis

Proper 23 / Pentecost 18 / Ordinary Time 28   185
Psalm 106:1-6, 19-23
Second Chances

Proper 24 / Pentecost 19 / Ordinary Time 29   189
Matthew 22:15-22
We Are, None of Us, Our Own

Proper 25 / Pentecost 20 / Ordinary Time 30   192
Matthew 22:34-46
Who's the Real Boss?

Reformation Day   195
John 8:31-36
Free Indeed

All Saints Day   201
Revelation 7:9-17
The Fifth Gospel

Proper 26 / Pentecost 21 / Ordinary Time 31   206
Psalm 107:1-7, 33-37
A Magical Little Poem

Proper 27 / Pentecost 22 / Ordinary Time 32   209
Joshua 24:1-3a, 14-25
As for Me and My House...

Proper 28 / Pentecost 23 / Ordinary Time 33   212
Matthew 25:14-30
Monster Dandruff

Christ the King (Proper 29) / Ordinary Time 34   214
Ezekiel 34:11-16, 20-24
Diamonds

Thanksgiving Day   217
Luke 17:11-19; Psalm 65
Thanksgiving

About the Authors   219

If You Like This Title...   223

Introduction

Since you are reading this, you probably preach on a regular basis. It is important to not only bring God's word to the members of your congregation but to help make the gospel of Christ engaging and thought-provoking.

Most people know that Jesus, the Master Storyteller, very often used stories and parables to make an important point to his listeners about God's kingdom. Following his example, we know that helping people to understand God's word through the telling of a story not only provides additional interest in a message, but also makes that same message easier to understand.

Over the years, CSS has published thousands of relevant, interesting, and inspiring anecdotes and stories to season a pastor's sermon. Not only has CSS produced numerous books to aid pastors in this important part of ministry but CSS also has a weekly online service called **StoryShare**, a component of **SermonSuite.com**, that was created to bring preachers the most timely and relevant illustrations possible. This edition of stories and anecdotes, gleaned from **StoryShare** for Cycle A, are written to dovetail with the readings from the Revised Common Lectionary and will serve you well as extended illustrations or in many cases, stand-alone sermons.

It is our hope that the stories in this book will not only assist you, the pastor, in your preaching but will also help you throughout your ministry.

The editors at CSS Publishing Company, Inc.

Advent 1
Matthew 24:36-44
by Peter Andrew Smith

Waiting in the Light

Carl set his bulging briefcase down just inside the entryway and shook the snow off his overcoat. Someone at the head office should have known about the sloppy accounting before they purchased the small business. Come to think of it, they must have had an idea since they stuck him with the job of sorting through the mess before the lawyers finished. He rubbed his head and hoped the aspirin started to work soon.

Carl enjoyed the silence for a moment. Sally must have convinced Mary to let her watch a video upstairs since it was too quiet for bedtime already. Maybe he could slip downstairs and make some headway on the financial records before they even noticed he was home.

He stopped short before he reached the bottom step. The normally tidy room was a disaster. Wrapping paper, tinsel, coloured lights, and Christmas decorations were strewn over every inch of floor space and flat surface.

"No, it's not in here," Sally said pushing a box out of the way before noticing him. "Daddy, you're home!"

"What is going on?" he asked.

"Aunt Mary and I are getting us ready for Christmas." She pointed at the string of lights snaking their way along the mantle. Her fingers worked a switch and the room lit up in multiple colours. "We have the lights all over the house. Isn't everything pretty?"

"You've made a mess!" Carl pulled the extension cord out of the wall and everything went dark. "How am I supposed to get any work done?"

Sally went very quiet and still.

Mary appeared from the storage room with a large box in her arms. "I think this one might have the rest of the nativity set."

Sally let out a wail and ran up the stairs.

"What did you say?" Mary asked him.

"Nothing."

"She wanted to put up the decorations for you as a surprise," Mary said. "I didn't think it was that big a deal."

Carl hefted the briefcase. "Things are really busy at work, and I need to get this done."

"This week."

"What?"

"There is always some reason for you being upset."

"Things will get better soon," Carl said. "It's just not a good time right now."

"When will be a good time?"

"Look, I said I was sorry. I'm doing the best I can as a single father."

Mary paused at the bottom of the stairs. "It's not me you need to apologize to. I'll send Sally down before she goes to bed."

Carl swept aside the decorations on the middle of the desk and went back to work. The numbers in this ledger didn't add up. He noticed something strange as he turned the page back and forth. Of course, two pages were stuck together.

He pulled them apart and an envelope fell into his lap. Carl opened it and saw the $10,000 bearer bond. He scanned down the new pages of the ledger and saw there was no record of it. Ten thousand dollars the former owner had forgotten about. He looked at the cheque that anyone could cash without question. Ten thousand dollars that the head office didn't know existed. He pushed his chair back. All he needed to do was forget to mention it in his final report. No one would be any the wiser. All his problems would be over.

Carl flipped on the desk lamp to examine the cheque and a partially assembled nativity scene appeared from the shadows. Joseph was standing all alone beside the manger. Carl looked at the carefully painted features on the man who had raised Jesus as his son. He had never noticed before that Joseph was smiling.

"Can I come in Daddy?" a tiny voice asked from the doorway. Carl opened his arms and his daughter rushed into them.

"I'm sorry," she said. "Please don't be mad or Jesus can't come at Christmas."

"I'm not mad," he replied. "And who told you that silly thing?"

Her face brightened. "You mean Jesus comes at Christmas no matter what?"

"Absolutely. The Bible tells us that nothing can stop Jesus from being with us." He kissed the top of her head. "Have a good sleep and maybe tomorrow when I come home we can put up the Christmas tree."

As Sally's footsteps retreated up the stairs, Carl held the figure of Joseph closer to the light and saw that the smile touched the eyes and rest of the face. The artist had captured not merely Joseph's joy but something else as well. Carl caught a glimpse of his own reflection in a piece of shiny wrapping paper. A frown and furrowed brow distorted by the shadows.

He put the smiling figure back under the light next to Jesus and picked up the envelope. No one would know if he kept the cheque for himself. He could give Sally the presents he always wanted to buy. He could hear her now excitedly telling her friends in Sunday school about Christmas morning. His heart sank. How could he go to church with Sally knowing what he had done? How could he raise her to follow Jesus if he turned away from God like this? How could he consider lying and cheating?

Carl set the envelope next to the nativity scene. He sent an email telling his boss about discovering the bearer bond along with an estimate of how many more days it was going to take to finish the audit.

On the way to the stairs, he stopped and plugged in the extension cord. The shriek of joy from Sally as all the Christmas decorations in the house lit up brought a smile to Carl's face. A smile very similar to the one an artist had been inspired to paint on the figure of Joseph for a nativity set.

Advent 2
Matthew 3:1-12
by David O. Bales

Repenting in the Friendly Skies

It wasn't how Clarence dressed. He long ago stopped wearing his clergy collar when traveling by air. He wore a simple suit and tie. To his wife's surprise, he even removed his cross necklace before entering the boarding area. Still, no matter if he needed the sleep or the time to arrange notes for a seminar, nearly every flight was filled with listening to his seatmate. While flying, he seemed the center of a magnetic field attracting people to him with their problems. He said, "I wonder if it's my aftershave?"

Last week Clarence had preached about his uncanny experiences on airplanes. "Often across half a continent I've heard about crimes, divorces, mean parents, faithless spouses, and rebellious children. I've shared tears and offered prayer. I always give my card and ask the person to report how life works out. However, more than fifty times in thirty years and never a response. For whatever spiritual gift God has granted me and for whatever purpose I'm supposed to employ it, when it comes to seatmates on airplanes, I become just a free ear."

This week Clarence flew to Denver. When he admitted to the woman beside him that he'd been a counselor in private practice for eleven years and was a pastor, she began to talk. "For twenty years I've been estranged from my brother." She pushed her fingers through her auburn hair and pressed on her head as though it hurt. "Right after my mom died he and his wife backed a truck up to her house and took everything. To this day my mom's china sits in my sister-in-law's cupboard and I know she doesn't use it."

"What have you done to be reconciled?"

"I was too stunned at the funeral. As soon as I got home I sent a letter saying how cruel they'd been to me."

"That's all?"

"I stopped sending Christmas and birthday cards."

"You haven't talked to them since the incident?"

"No. But my cousin tells me what they're saying about me."

"And you want my advice?"

"Sure do."

"If it's your style to send letters instead of speaking in person, write another. Be very specific. Write that you're sorry for the decades of silence between you. He's your brother and you're sorry that you cut off the relationship and you want to be reconciled."

She yanked her head back in surprise, her eyes enlarged. The plane bumped and she gulped. "And then?"

"Then you wait for his reply. If you don't get one in a month, write the same letter but add that you beg him to be reconciled."

"No," she said, shaking her head, "I mean then don't I put something in the letter about his returning what he stole from me?"

"Nothing more."

Her jaw muscles bulged. A baby cried and they both looked up. Then she lifted her book and read. Soon, with a grumpy look on her face, she slept. An hour later she woke. She turned to Clarence as though picking up the conversation mid-sentence, "You mean I let my brother go free. Just let him have mom's stuff?"

Clarence leaned toward her, "Have you talked to other counselors about this?"

"Yes."

"How many and for how many years?"

"You mean how many total years did I meet with a counselor?"

"How many years from when you started with the first one and finished with the last one?"

"Thirteen or fourteen years, I think."

"Have you settled the problem?"

"Not too well."

"Did any counselor suggest you seek reconciliation or to begin by confessing your own sin?"

"You don't even know me," she blinked with a wince, "and you're suggesting I confess my sins."

"You don't even know me and you're telling me your problems."

She opened her mouth but Clarence spoke, "Every problem has two sides. That's obvious, but God wants us to be reconciled. All the families Jesus told about were dysfunctional. Even if your brother is 95% wrong, you need to set out, without your being 100% right, to become reconciled."

"But, but —"

"No buts," Clarence said. "The only time Jesus was approached to settle an inheritance between family members he warned about greed, instead. I think it's because we humans blame others and excuse ourselves. Certainly some people are emotionally beaten. They think too little of themselves. But mostly we blame others." He raised his voice, "Brothers and sisters blame each other. Children blame parents. Parents," his voice caught, but he continued, "blame children. We all need to clean up our relationships with one another and with God by confessing our part in the problem."

She listened but didn't respond.

"You asked my advice," he said, "and that's it."

An hour later as she stood to deplane she nodded to Clarence. He said, "I wish the best for you and your brother."

When Clarence reached the baggage area he spotted Bradley: auburn hair about the same length as his seatmate's, T-shirt, holes in the knees of his jeans, and wearing flip-flops. Clarence suddenly felt the weight of his suit.

"Hello, son," Clarence said and held out his hand.

Bradley looked surprised and held out his, "Hello, Father."

"Thanks for agreeing to ferry me to the seminar."

"I usually can break free in the middle of the day." He turned away from his father toward the baggage carousel as he spoke, "How many suitcases you got?"

"Two. One's clothes. The other's super-heavy — the projector, books, and handouts. But I'm not concerned about those right now. Is there a coffee shop or something near?"

"Right off the freeway, about a mile, Red's."

"If you've got time, let's go there. I'll buy you coffee. I've had an interesting flight. Thought about you and me. There's something I want to talk to you about."

Advent 3
James 5:7-10
by Rick McCracken-Bennett

Lessons of a Farmer

Anyone who has grown up on a farm knows that there are many lessons that a person can learn if he or she just keeps his/her eyes and ears and heart open. This is a story about a young boy who does just that.

> *Be patient, therefore, beloved, until the coming of the Lord. The farmer waits for the precious crop from the earth, being patient with it until it receives the early and the late rains. You also must be patient. Strengthen your hearts, for the coming of the Lord is near. Beloved, do not grumble against one another, so that you may not be judged. See, the Judge is standing at the doors! As an example of suffering and patience, beloved, take the prophets who spoke in the name of the Lord.*
> — James 5:7-10

If you keep your eyes and ears open you can learn a lot growing up on a farm. David O'Malley did. Just ask his dad. Or his grandpa.

David was one of those boys who just loved to follow his dad and his grandpa around wherever they went and whatever they happened to be doing. If they were feeding the pigs (slopping the hogs, his grandpa called it) or plowing and disking the fields, David wanted to be with them and begged and pleaded until they gave in and took him along.

As he grew older he tried to help. He was always trying to do farm work even though the finer points of hog slopping and egg gathering eluded him much of the time. His dad and grandpa were patient... well, most of the time, as they tried to show him how to slop the pigs without getting more slop on him than he got in the trough.

One day David was tooling around the farm (as his grandpa used to describe him). After a while, his father began to wonder what he might be getting into in the way that a nine-year-old can get into things. All at once, he heard a racket in the henhouse. He ran across the barnyard, pulled open the door just in time to find David, surrounded by broken eggs, shaking an egg, holding it up to his ear, and then bending down and breaking it open on the floor, much to the dismay, it seemed, of several of the hens. "What in the world do you think you're doing?"

"I'm trying to let the chicks out, Dad," he said as he went for another egg.

"No you don't," his dad said, biting his lip to keep from laughing. "Come here and let's clean up this mess and I'll tell you why that didn't work."

Yes, you can learn lots of things on a farm, if you keep your eyes and ears open.

One afternoon David's dad turned his back for just one minute and David was gone. Now this was in the days before you would think the worst when something like that happened, and so his dad took his time looking around the farm for him.

"What in the name of all that is holy do you think you're doing?" he shouted when he found his son lying on the ground next to two of the farm dogs who were, shall we say, being quite friendly with each other.

"I'm just trying to see what the dogs are fighting about but I can't tell, Daddy."

It was time for biting lips once again and for the first of many talks about the birds and the bees.

David turned ten in the spring and "helped" his grandpa and his dad plant the corn. Every night or so his dad would take him out to the edge of the field behind their house and show him how the corn was sprouting and then beginning to raise up shoots out of the ground. The rains were good that year and it wasn't long before the field took on the look of a bona fide cornfield.

One night after supper, David's dad walked to the field by himself only to find David already there. He stood a ways back and watched as his son stooped down, pulled out a stalk of corn, looked at the roots, and then threw the stalk away. Then he stooped down and repeated the process.

"What do you think you're doing?"

"I want to see if the corn is growing," David said matter-of-factly.

It was time for another lesson about farming. "Son, sit down here. You know, the most important thing you need to know about being a farmer is that you need patience. We plow the fields and scatter grain, as that old song reminds us, but then God sends the rain and God makes it all grow. There is a point in all that when you and I just have to step back and wait for God to take our good work and turn it into a harvest. You can pull up all the stalks you want, but you won't make it grow any faster and, in fact, you'll actually hurt the crop. Farming is all about trusting God to do what God is supposed to do. The harvest will come in God's good time. Do you understand that?"

"I think so," David said as he gazed with the eyes of a budding farmer at his dad's field.

Yes, if you keep your eyes and ears open you can learn a lot on a farm. You can even learn a lot about God.

Advent 4
Matthew 1:18-25
by C. David McKirachan

I'm Pregnant

I'd been married two months. I was working at a church in the inner city. My last paycheck had to wait until they'd counted the change from the Coke machine. It was one of our best moneymakers. My new wife and I had plans. We were going to keep our present positions for a while. She received a paycheck that did not depend on a Coke machine. Then we'd take our time finding a more beaucolic environment, where muggings were not part of the commute. Then we'd work on kids. Good plan.

She came bouncing into the kitchen and announced with glee, "I'm pregnant."

Thank God she then danced out of the room and upstairs to inform the important people on her address list. I worked on getting a breath. Then I descended into the basement. I don't mean emotionally, I mean I went down the steps. The basement of the manse was rather scary. It flooded most times it rained. It was moldy and things moved when you turned off the lights. I was not a fan of the basement. I went there as little as possible. Today it seemed like the place to go.

High on the moldy walls were windows about eighteen inches from sill to top. I stood there looking at the one above the sink. I carefully reasoned that if I climbed up on the slimy gray edge and managed not to slip, I could probably yank out the nails that were our security system. Then I could squeeze through.

It took me a few minutes to find the tracks of sanity in the swamp of craziness. The first indication that I was thinking again was the realization that it would be a lot easier to walk out the front door. There, next to the slimy sink was one of the most insane bits of my life. It was hard to breathe in the dank and moldy dimness. But I managed a few deep breaths and came to the conclusion that plan or no plan, I was going to be a father. Wow! After the basement moment, the rest of it was rather cool. Fathers don't have to deal with morning sickness or labor. That's why we can say that.

We all cruise through the Christmas story forgetting that these people were real. I realize Joseph probably didn't have a basement. I realize the social dynamics were different. But who with a brain in their head is ever totally prepared to hear those two words, "I'm pregnant"? I betcha' he had to breathe deeply more than a couple of times before he could get himself wrapped around that one — especially with the whole Holy Spirit thing. Being a father is enough. Being a father of a child of the Holy Spirit... I'd say he needed a basement.

I'm not embarrassed about my basement moment. It was very honest and decisional. Down there in the nastiest place I could find, I got a grip on the most important thing I'd ever have to lift. I also realized, I couldn't lift it by myself. None of us can. All kids are children of the Holy Spirit. They come into our lives from somewhere else and alter our existence forever. They change us. They change the world. We can't take credit for them. They belong to themselves and to God. Our job is to listen to the whisper of dreams, to the angels who say improbable things to us. Our job is to believe that in spite of all our limitations and fears, we've got something to give to this unknown person who is coming soon.

I named him Jonathan, "Gift of God." His middle name is David, "Beloved." He's my son. I know Joseph was proud. Just like I was, after I came out of the basement.

"For unto us a child is born, unto us a son is given."

A Merry Christmas to you all.

Christmas Eve / Day
Luke 2:1-14
by Stan Purdum

The Great Christmas-Tree Battle

On a particular Saturday, just nine days before their first Christmas together, Archie was at his desk working on one of his grad school assignments when Annie came home from Christmas shopping.

Annie's greeting to her husband was "When are we going to put up the tree?"

Ah yes, the tree, Archie thought. Some weeks earlier Annie had suggested purchasing an artificial tree, but he'd made a big fuss about having a real tree. So Annie gave in and the couple bought a real tree. It was leaning against the side of their house at that very moment. It had been leaning there for a week already.

But now Archie regretted his insistence. He made some sounds about his homework not going well and suggested putting off dealing with the tree until some indefinite "later."

"Such as when?" Annie asked. "You go to school all week. We need to do it today."

Knowing that in marital impasses of this sort, discretion is indeed the better part of valor, Archie reluctantly abandoned his assignment and donned old clothes. He armed himself with gloves, a hatchet, saw, hammer, spikes, wire and wire cutters, and then retrieved the tree. Annie brought out a little tree stand she'd picked up while shopping.

Looking at the tree, it all seemed easy enough. The stand slipped easily onto the base of the tree without Archie even having to lop of any branches. Triumphantly, he carried the whole business into the house and stood it in front of the picture window.

It looked pretty nice — until it fell over a moment later.

The next 45 minutes were spent in a desperate struggle involving branch trimming, readjusting of the stand and the assembling of a network of wires, which, if electrified, would have provided power for the entire community. The battle ended with Archie driving a spike right through the bottom of the stand into the base of the tree — but to no avail. The blasted thing still wouldn't remain upright. (And at that point, Archie began to have some very unkind thoughts about Martin Luther, who, according to legend, began the entire Christmas tree practice.)

In disgust, Archie finally drove to a hardware store and explained his problem to the proprietor. The proprietor showed Archie a few stands, but they were all similar to the one he already had. Then the man said, "Actually, I've got just the thing in the storeroom," and he motioned Archie to follow him. There he picked up a monstrous contraption consisting of a huge pan with grappling hooks and turnbuckles attached. "This," he said, "is the tree stand we used ourselves. We switched to an artificial tree a few years ago so we don't need this anymore. It will hold up any tree." Then he gave the stand to Archie for nothing.

Back home, Archie first had to remove from the tree the stand Annie had bought, no simple task because of the spike he'd pounded through it. In fact, Archie had to destroy the stand to get it off and worse, he had to leave the large nail imbedded in the bottom of the tree. This nail, in turn, meant that he had to place the tree off-center in the new stand. Thus, it took Archie fully another hour of fierce combat to get the tree situated in the new stand, but he finally succeeded. Gingerly, he placed the tree in the designed spot, and then he called Annie in to see it.

"That looks pretty nice," Annie said, "but this side needs to go toward the window." Obligingly, Archie turned the tree and was horrified to see the stand come off. (At that point, Archie began to have some very unkind thoughts about Annie.)

Another hour's work, and Archie finally got the darn thing up again, this time facing the direction Annie wanted. The tree remained staunchly upright for the remainder of the holiday season.

A couple of days after his great battle with the Christmas tree, Archie ran into the hardware store proprietor on the street. The man asked Archie if the stand had worked. Archie indicated that he'd had "a little difficulty," but admitted that in the end, it did the job.

The man chuckled and then said, "By the way, I remember now why we switched to an artificial tree. It was because of the big fight my wife and I had every year when we tried to put up a real tree using that stand."

"Thanks a lot!" Archie said.

The man replied, "Yeah, that stand is kind of tough to use, but the main reason I switched to an artificial tree is because in the struggle with the real tree, I forgot that the reason we decorate our homes is for a birthday party for Someone special. So I wanted to celebrate it without resentment over some darn tree. I wanted what I did to get the house ready to be an act of appreciation for the Birthday Boy.

Christmas 1
Matthew 2:13-23
by Peter Andrew Smith

God With Us

Mary tensed as the nurse passed by the door of the waiting room. Before she could ask the woman shook her head slightly in response, smiled at the sight of Joshua curled up in a chair clutching his teddy bear, and continued down the hallway. Mary forced herself to sit back in the chair and relax.

She took another drink of the vending machine coffee and sighed. Some Christmas this was turning into. A frantic phone call that her father had been taken to the emergency room, a six hour drive through lousy weather, and then stuck in this room waiting for a doctor to speak to her.

"Mommy, is it Christmas yet?" Joshua said sleepily.

"No, baby go back to sleep."

Thankfully he closed his eyes and drifted off again. She didn't want a repeat of the panic when she woke him up to get them on the road. He didn't understand what was happening and cried when she told him they had to go right now. She wished she believed the words she had used to convince him that everything would be okay.

The clock on the wall said 2:30 am. Technically it was Christmas Day but she didn't want to tell that to her son. She didn't need to see his disappointment that there were no presents, no stocking full of goodies, and no cheerful decorations other than the tired piece of artificial greenery strung over the door of the empty hospital waiting room. She couldn't handle that on top of not knowing what was happening with her father.

The nurse reappeared at the door with a small stocking filled with candy. "It's not much."

Mary smiled. "It's something."

"Can I get you anything?" the nurse asked. "Coffee?"

Mary shook her head. "Do you know how much longer the doctor will be?"

The nurse shrugged and Mary returned to her seat.

"Mommy, is it Christmas?" Joshua asked stirring beside her.

"Not yet," Mary said. At least she could postpone his disappointment for a couple of more hours.

His eyes went wide as he saw the stocking. "Is that for me?"

"Sure," she said handing it to him.

He dug through the treasures of foil coated chocolates and found a candy cane. She started to tell him to only take one piece when a man with a stethoscope wrapped around his neck walked past the door. Mary sprang to her feet and rushed into the hallway.

"That's his daughter there," the nurse said pointing at Mary.

The doctor introduced himself and went into a long description of what had happened to her father and what tests they were running on him. Mary couldn't follow most of it.

"Is he going to be okay?" she asked.

"It's too early to be sure but he is responding to the medications. We'll know more after the tests come back." The man smiled weakly. "I'm sorry I wish I could tell you more but right now we just don't know."

"I understand. Is it okay if I take my son in to see him?"

The doctor said that would be fine and Mary turned back to the waiting room. She started to rehearse what she was going to tell Joshua about what he would see and how his beloved Grampy was doing. The stocking was sitting on the chair along with his coat and teddy bear but Joshua was nowhere to be seen.

Mary looked up and down the deserted hallway. She started toward the nurses' station when she heard a faint voice singing.

"Happy Birthday to you... Happy Birthday, baby Jesus. Happy Birthday to you."

She turned the corner to see Joshua take a candy cane from his pocket and put it into the manger of the nativity scene set up in an alcove.

"Sorry, it is not much of a birthday present, baby Jesus. Mommy and I had to come here because Grampy is really sick. Please help him and Mommy, okay?"

The scolding she was going to give Joshua for disappearing caught in her throat and she simply said his name.

"Hi Mommy." He yawned. "The nurse told me it was Christmas."

"It is," she said. "We can't open up any presents though until we go home and I don't know when that will be."

"Okay," Joshua said his face very serious. "Can I see Grampy now?"

"You can but he is sleeping and there are lots of wires and equipment like we sometimes see on television so the doctors can help him get better." Mary took his hand. "Do you still want to see him?"

Joshua nodded.

"I'm sorry this isn't much of a Christmas," Mary said softly.

"But you told me Grampy needed us to be here," Joshua said. "And you told me that Christmas isn't about presents but about the baby Jesus being born because God loves us."

"It is."

"So why isn't this a good Christmas?" His face fell. "Was I supposed to wait to sing happy birthday to the baby Jesus until you were here?"

"No," she said letting his words echo in her head and heart. A hospital was not where she wanted to be this Christmas but she knew they needed to be here. She knelt down to speak to him face-to-face. "You have been a great help to Mommy. A little angel."

A huge grin broke out on his face. "Really?"

"Absolutely," Mary said. As she took Joshua in her arms she felt an embrace of love and peace, which she knew would hold her through this difficult time. As they started back toward intensive care she whispered a prayer of thanks.

New Year's Day
Ecclesiastes 3:1-13
by David O. Bales

Christina-Kay's Grandfather

Cameron ran into the kitchen, "If I could wish anything for a youth pastor, it would be Christina-Kay." Angela leaned her pregnant stomach against the counter and sprinkled cheese onto the salad. "I wondered if you'd established your legal address at the church building."

"I'm sorry, Hon. It was a great youth group."

He put his Bible on top of the refrigerator and dashed to the table with dishes and cutlery. "A kid who believes and asks questions, who'll listen to Robert quote scripture he doesn't understand, and yet be kind to him — there aren't many high school juniors that mature."

"I asked her on Sunday when the baby's born," Angela said, patting her stomach, "if she'd babysit for us. She was pleased."

Christina-Kay could ask Cameron or Angela to loan her $100 and they'd do it without question. Consequently, when she told Cameron the next week that her grandfather was now living with them and was ill and she'd like Cameron to visit, he agreed without a thought.

Christina-Kay led Cameron into the living room. He wasn't surprised that her mother wasn't there. Since her divorce she put too much responsibility on Christina-Kay.

Mr. Renaunt sat in a recliner. He was thin and bald except for two white sideburns puffing out like cotton balls. He smiled weakly and slowly held up his hand. As he did, he dropped a magazine. "Nice to meet you, Reverend. I'd get up, but by the time I did, it would —"

Cameron sat on the couch next to him. "That's okay."

"Grandpa, you sit," Christina-Kay said. She kissed him on the cheek. "Cam, I gotta get back to school. Mom's at the store. Just let yourself out when you are done."

"See you, kid," Cameron said as she left.

"What a grandkid you've got there, Mr. Renaunt."

"She's wonderful, and... and..." He looked at the floor and paused. "Might as well get right to it. She wants you to meet me because you'll probably do my funeral, and pretty soon."

"I'm sorry, Mr. Renaunt."

Mr. Renaunt glanced at Cameron, "I'm not happy to end this way — it's my liver, nothing left of it — but I'm resigned." He coughed. "But, I'll say it and save you time." He placed his bony hand upon Cameron's. "I mean you no disrespect, son, but I don't believe."

Cameron looked surprised.

Mr. Renaunt leaned back in his chair and closed his eyes, "I mean you no disrespect. I just don't believe what you do."

"About God."

"Yes. I've been around a lot of good people and I like the idea of God." He rested his head on the chair back but opened his eyes, looking up. "I look at the world and it had to come from somewhere. But a personal God...."

They talked for half an hour about the world's beauty and order and about suffering and tragedies. They shared their perceptions and experiences. Cameron spoke quietly, "I can't argue you into faith, Mr. Renaunt. I won't try. I appreciate your honesty. And I mean no disrespect, but I'll be praying for you. If you need any spiritual comfort or if you want to discuss the Christian faith, I'll be here for you."

"Thank you," Mr. Renaunt said and again closed his eyes, "but I don't think I will."

Over the next month, the older and younger man each proved good to their word. Mr. Renaunt didn't ask to speak with Cameron and Cameron prayed for Mr. Renaunt.

Cameron arrived at the funeral home to make arrangements for the memorial. He wasn't surprised that only Christina-Kay met him. She cried when Cameron walked in. He hugged her and cried also. The funeral director left the two alone. Christina-Kay never completely stopped crying, "You know Grandpa didn't believe." She held up her chin as if defending him.

"Christina-Kay," Cameron began slowly, "I know this is difficult for you —"

"This isn't about me," she said. She looked angry through her tears. "Mom's worried." She bit her upper lip and breathed in deeply. "This is about you and what you're going to say about Grandpa."

Cameron jerked his head back, "I can't say he believed."

She shook her head quickly side to side. "That's not all. I phoned Dad and he's coming. He'll stay away from Mom and he'll be okay, but he doesn't believe either. He's still mad at his parents for forcing church on him."

Cameron reached to touch her, but she pulled away. "I just wish that faith and who has it and who doesn't wasn't so important." She was crying hard again, "You said the Bible is broad as well as deep, Cam. If God's as good as you say, isn't there any place in heaven for Grandpa?"

Cameron began two days of agonizing. At the memorial service he was numb from lack of sleep. After prayers and obituary he read Ecclesiastes 3:1-13 and said, "Notice that even when verses 9-13 speak of God, God is distant. Verses 1-8 scrawl items onto the list of life's repetitions. Ecclesiastes lays these realities before us, telling us the truth — the pleasant and the hard. Ecclesiastes courageously admits life's catastrophes and honestly acknowledges its joys. For him life is a river flowing between the banks of opposites. During our whole journey we float from one bank to the other, but constantly downstream. In this voyage, God isn't always visible. But if one cannot believe, as does the rest of the Bible, that life's 'aimed' — that it came from somewhere and is going somewhere — at least one can recognize as did Ecclesiastes and Maurice Renaunt — that life is ordered.

That's not a full, Christian faith, but it's a faith the Bible records for us. As we face the loss of our loved one, let's trust that Ecclesiastes wouldn't be included in the Bible if God doesn't acknowledge that faith.

Christmas 2
Ephesians 1:3-14
by C. David McKirachan

You Were Adopted

In some ways I had a very strange childhood. Most preacher's kids do. But there is very little in that strange childhood that I would trade for something further toward the cultural mean. Yet there were moments when I was treated like a normal kid. I had siblings much older than myself, so they had more responsibility for the brat than they would have preferred. Once in a while the kid brother got treated like any other kid brother.

I remember one such day clearly. Having done my best to be a pain in the neck and other parts of the anatomy, I was given a secret. All little kids love secrets. My sister sat me down and very seriously whispered to me, "Did you know you're adopted?" I had no idea what that meant but seeking to seem wise I shook my head, "No." My sister smiled. That was good, so I continued, "I had no idea." Then she laughed. It wasn't the laugh of a larger person putting down a smaller person, a laugh of domination and cruelty. It was a laugh of a big sister thinking her little brother was cute.

Later I asked the well of all practical knowledge, my mother, "What's adopted?" She descended on the question like a hawk on an unsuspecting gerbil.

"Where did you hear that?" I told her and she worked hard at not being horrified rather unsuccessfully. But then I got the "precious" speech, which included bits and pieces from the labor and delivery saga of one Charles David McKirachan. In other words, NO WAY, I WAS THERE!

Though she was not happy about the whole thing, I thought the conversation was great. When I finally got a clear definition of "adopted" it still had that valence of special and kind of cool. They had worked so hard making it not a bad thing that it never occurred to me that it might be. My father being cued into the conversation went into a word study of the first chapter of Ephesians at dinner. Like I said, I had a weird childhood.

The part of the word study I understood came down on the "special" business even more solidly. I began to get jealous of these special people who'd had the privilege of being chosen rather than pushed out. I also remember the first time I met an adoptee. I told them it must be really cool to have that privilege. They weren't interested in Ephesians.

Paul agrees with me. Adoption, for him like any self-respecting Hebrew/educated Greek, meant you were solidly included in the clan and eligible for inheritance. Pretty cool. Now how many times can anybody say with certitude that Paul agrees with them? I don't know when older siblings got off on the wrong track and started making it second class to be included like this.

There are a lot of kids not to mention animals waiting to be treated as special. I think they would agree with Paul too. It's pretty cool to be brought into the family.

Hey, if God liked the strategy, who is dumb enough to disagree with him?

I doubt my sister saw it that way after my mother got through with her.

Epiphany of Our Lord
Matthew 2:1-12
by Scott Dalgarno

The Bethlehem Conundrum

In the time of King Herod, after Jesus was born in Bethlehem, wise men from the east came to Jerusalem asking, "Where is the child who has been born king of the Jews?"

— Matthew 2:1-2

Let's see, what's a Magi? Are these wise men or astrologers or kings? This is the Bethlehem conundrum.

Well, the real Bethlehem conundrum is the subterfuge of King Herod posing as someone anxious to bow down and worship the Christ Child. The wise kings travel untold leagues to visit the baby, and Herod won't travel eight miles down the Bethlehem road before lunch to take a look for himself. And we know what he's driven by, don't we? It's certainly not devotion.

Right here, in the heart of Matthew's Christmas story, is a jealous king plotting a murder. What happened to the peace of "Silent Night"?

Eight Februarys ago, I had the incredible fortune to travel to Israel. I remember so well our visit to Bethlehem, what Isaiah the prophet called the city of David. That day, before tensions between Israelis and Palestinians began to rise, one could still imagine an impossibly young Palestinian girl, literally filled with holy purpose, astride a donkey going down that little town's one main street looking desperately, by starlight, for "the" (singular) inn. Our own visit seemed anything but momentous. We took our time to examine the stones of the floor of the original church planted there under the direction of Constantine's devout mother, Saint Helena.

We then made our way down below the central altar to the first-century grotto where the baby was supposed to have been born. I remember being moved most by the humble cell, there still, where Saint Jerome translated the Vulgate, just a few feet away from the scene of the original manger. How remarkable for one like him to work and worship there daily, hourly, minute by minute. It must have been like living in the middle of a meditation. How powerful, but nothing prepared me for what I met upon coming back up to the level of the modern church.

Rapidly lengthening shadows eclipsed the intense sunlight that only a moment before had been streaming through the rear doors. This was followed by the sound of dozens of swift steps on stone. A score, then two figures, all in black, entered the church followed by four men carrying what looked like a very plane wooden coffin. The sound of it being placed down on the limestone floor before the altar was startling, deep, and dry. This was definitely no museum of the nativity. Though there were thirty or more of us milling about the place, the worshipers, obviously moved by this one's passing, ignored us completely. No doubt about it, this was every bit a living church; a faithful, tight (albeit ancient) Christian community very much in mourning.

Feeling terribly obtrusive, I wanted to just disappear; yet, I was transfixed. How perfect, I thought. The integrity of the church at Bethlehem, one of the oldest churches in Christendom, was this minute clear for anyone with eyes to see. Here, 2,000 years along, this ancient shrine so faithfully served to shelter the celebration of a Christian's death. Within minutes, the service was over, and, just as swiftly, the mourners hurried out, on their way, no doubt, to the local cemetery to tuck away this loved one.

How ironic. We had come in search of one thing and found something utterly, profoundly different. Bethlehem, the place of Christ's birth, had given us a glimpse of what a truly holy death should look like. And by attending to the tenderness and honor attached to that anonymous Palestinian's death we had come more deeply to appreciate the holy birth of the most famous human being in our planet's history, someone pilgrims have journeyed to Bethlehem to honor for some 1,800 years.

A holy birth and a holy death; what are they separated by? A few steps. A few holy steps. But looking in at Matthew's version of the nativity — it's not strange at all. Christmas is barely five days gone and here, in this gospel, just twelve verses past the nativity is the insertion of the story of King Herod's massacre of the boy babies in Bethlehem.

King Herod "The Great" threatened by talk of a new king, will order the killing of all the boy babies around the little town. Down through the ages innumerable kings and dictators have ordered the massacre of Jewish children. It's an old story and is so in contrast with "O Little Town of Bethlehem, how still we see they lie." Still in death, maybe.

So, Matthew's Christmas pageant will end not with tinsel covered angels proclaiming goodwill, but Rachel weeping for her slaughtered children. Christmas in Bethlehem, the real Bethlehem.

Herod was no fool. He had been in power long enough to be able to tell a rival when he saw one. What dirty shepherds saw as a baby, a distant relative of King David, Herod knew as a threat to everything on which his kingdom was based.

So Herod joins all the other leaders of our age, Hitler, Pol Pot, Stalin, Mao, Milosevic (and perhaps Musharraf?); men who didn't mind a little murder in order to advance their political ideals, however evil or wrong-headed.

The Magi in T.S. Eliot's poem, "Journey of the Magi," ask, "Were we led all that way for Birth or Death? There was a Birth, certainly. We had evidence and no doubt. I had seen birth and death, but had thought they were different; this birth was hard and bitter agony for us, like death, our death. We returned to our places, these Kingdoms, but no longer at ease here, in the old dispensation, with an alien people clutching their gods."[1]

So it is for all men and women who find the new kingdom of Jesus wearying. But I sense that the old Magi went back to their homes feeling more like Simeon in Luke's wonderful after-Christmas story, happy to have been granted long enough life to recognize real hope when they saw it in the face.

---

1. T.S. Eliot, *Collected Poems, 1909-1962* (San Diego, California: Harcourt Trade Publishers, 1991), pp. 99-100.

Baptism of Our Lord / Epiphany 1 / Ordinary Time 1
Isaiah 42:1-9; Acts 10:34-43
by Argile Smith

Welcoming Mr. Forsythe

Mr. Forsythe made his work as an elementary school principal look easy. He had a knack for managing his swarm of teachers, coaches, administrators, students, and parents so that teaching and learning could happen every school day. Even though he didn't try to rule with an iron hand, everyone seemed to have tremendous respect for him.

He certainly didn't look like a top-shelf administrator. Not a tall man at all, he had a few strands of unruly gray hair on the top of his head with a little more hanging on for dear life around his hat line. A portly fellow, he cut a heavy-in-the-middle figure that would remind you of Santa Claus, and he always looked like he had been dressed by committee. Nothing he wore seemed to match really well or fit quite right. His signature accessory to his garbled wardrobe happened to be a pair of thick glasses that perched precariously on the end of his nose all the time.

Mr. Forsythe had incredible power over the school. Teachers lived with the reality that he could fire and replace each one of them as he deemed necessary. Students knew that the stroke of his pen could have them imprisoned to detention, Saturday school, or worse. Parents learned that he had the clout to make things happen. Every member of the school board understood the depth of his influence in the community.

But power didn't matter to him very much. The children in his school, however, meant the world to him. He cared deeply about them — each one of them.

For instance, he liked to drop by the third-grade classes and quiz the students on their multiplication tables. All third-graders should have a firm grip on everything from "two times one" to "nine times nine" as far as he was concerned. That's why he would arrange "surprise" visits to each of the third-grade classes.

On a typical surprise visit, he would say to the teacher, "I dropped by to see if these students were as smart as the other third-grade classes." Then he would ask, "Would you mind if I asked a few questions?"

That's when the fun would begin. He would walk down the aisles, point to a student at random, and throw out a question like, "Two times seven?" A correct answer got a hearty, "Great!" Answering incorrectly got an encouraging "you'll get it next time" reply. Up and down the aisle he would go, hurling multiplication table questions left and right. Then he would leave, thanking the teacher for allowing him to interrupt and adding so everyone could hear, "They're really smart, aren't they?"

One day he made a surprise visit to a class in which Charlie sat quietly trying to deal with a toothache. Charlie came from a poor family that couldn't afford dental care. He didn't wear nice clothes either, and he knew it. In fact, Charlie spent much of his time at school trying to be invisible. To make matters worse, his tooth hurt on the very day Mr. Forsythe made one of his surprise visits his class.

In usual fashion, Mr. Forsythe made his way up and down the aisle and quizzed one student after another, getting closer to Charlie with each step he took. Then he flashed the question at Charlie, "Six times nine?"

Forgetting his pain for a split second, Charlie spoke up, "Fifty-four."

Then Mr. Forsythe launched a follow-up query, "Nine times eight?"

"Seventy-two!" Charlie shot back.

"You're good." Mr. Forsythe said. Then he turned to the teacher and confirmed, "He's really good."

After Mr. Forsythe left the classroom, Charlie thought about Mr. Forsythe's visit. The most powerful person in his third-grade world had just said in public that he mattered. For a while, his tooth stopped hurting, and his self-esteem healed a little too. As far as he was concerned, Mr. Forsythe could visit his classroom anytime.

Jesus came, powerful yet gentle and caring. People who know him that way always welcome Him into their lives.

Epiphany 2 / Ordinary Time 2
John 1:29-42
by C. David McKirachan

Too Close for Comfort

Seeing is a different opportunity than it used to be. In this latter day, we "see" through technology. We are invited to be voyeurs, one step back from what is going on through the tube or on the other side of the internet or up there on the other side of the rainbow of the big screen. Seeing has become a largely passive operation.

To see in former times, one had to be in the vicinity of the situation being seen. To be a witness was to be there, literally. One had to be in the thick of it to get a view close enough to see what was going on, there were no satellite links or cell phones that did video.

The other day I watched a football game that hung on the call of the referee. The commentators, having watched the play backward and forward from every angle imaginable, came to the conclusion that the ref was wrong and therefore the game that followed didn't really portray the "real" winner and loser. It's obvious that our senses aren't dependable as we participate in a situation. We need to have some sort of back up that will allow us to be at least a few rows away to get a better view. I mean after all, we might get confused or involved or maybe even emotionally influenced by what was going on around us. Better set up those links. We might not be seeing what we think we see.

Part of our confirmation process is unpacking the Sunday service. They bang the sermon and the worship experience around from their own perspective and hear ours. It's called interactive learning. During Advent one of them made the comment, "I didn't really like the music we had today. It was kind of weird. It sounded like... ancient. But," here he smiled, "it made the hair stand up on the back of my neck." Obviously, he wasn't "listening" objectively. Obviously, he was too involved in a manipulative situation to make a judgment about what was going on. Poor boy. He should learn to listen to the instant replay. It's much more dependable.

When Jesus told his visitors to "Come and see," he was suckering them into a situation. He was seducing them, sneaking up on them, nudging them toward one of those experiences when the hair stands up on the back of your neck. Those experiences are some of the most important experiences in our lives. "Observing" our religion from a distance just isn't enough. We are invited to come and see right up close and personal. We are invited to leave our objectivity at the door and get into the thick of it. Probably we won't understand or make sense of the best of it. We might even get a little frightened or awed. We might get uncomfortable. Angels tend to do that to people. I wonder what they look like on an instant replay?

Epiphany 3 / Ordinary Time 3
Isaiah 9:1-4
by Frank Ramirez

One Bright Light

The people who walked in darkness have seen a great light; those who lived in a land of deep darkness — on them light has shined.
— Isaiah 9:2

It's not easy to get to Chaco Culture National Historical Park. Located in the northwest corner of New Mexico, it's an isolated part of an isolated state. You turn off a lonely two-lane highway to drive another twenty miles down a largely unimproved road.

Bring along whatever food or shelter you think you'll need, because there are no hotels, motels, or even soft-sided cabins, but there is a campground for you to pitch your tent. Water is available if you run out, which is good, because it gets awfully hot there in the summer — and terribly cold in the winter.

Chaco Canyon might get ten inches of rain a year — in a good year. From the Visitor Center — very informative though not particularly large — you drive out to the canyon itself. The Fajada Butte is a recognizable landmark. A sluggish creek might run through the Chaco Wash if there is water. The forbidding cliffs rise on both sides.

Why take such trouble to get to this isolated place? Because a thousand years ago this was the center of the universe for the Anasazi people. From this place a web of roads spread out, straight and true, in all directions. Bells from Oregon, Macaws from Mexico, pottery from east as far as the

Great Plains, and west all the way to the coast, a wonderful traffic of goods passed through here.

Corn was planted on every available plot of land with the hope that some of it at least would drink deeply of the sparse rains that fell. Every plant in the desert environment had a use. Turkeys provided eggs and feathers, dogs provided protection for the valuable turkeys and other valuable goods, and the people, whose excavated teeth tell vivid stories of good crops and famine as accurately as tree rings chart the passing years, hunted, gathered, harvested, and most of all — built.

Here in Chaco Canyon are the ruins of buildings larger than anything that would be found in North America or Europe until the late nineteenth century. No one knows what language these people spoke or their names for the places they left behind, but later explorers discovered Pueblo Bonito, four to five stories high with over 600 rooms and over twenty of the rooms known to later Puebloans as Kivas, where dance and worship and ritual mixed together. Each of the Great Houses, as they are known, took centuries to build. Thanks to dendrochronology, the science of dating by tree rings, researchers can pinpoint what year each addition to each of the Great Houses was built.

A little past Pueblo Bonito there is a six-and-a-half mile round trip hike to the Penasco Blanco ruins. The walk would be worth it just for the opportunity to walk by a series of petroglyphs along one rock face and to walk among the ruins. But near the end of the trail there is a half-mile detour that reads: "Supernova Pictograph."

There, on an overhang providing next to no shelter on a rock face, is a simple painting.

There is a hand, a crescent moon, and a many-rayed star.

On July 4, 1054, the crescent moon would have risen in the predawn eastern sky. It is quite possible that some of the

Anasazi would already be up, working hard before the heat of the day made such labor difficult. The sky was very important to these ancient people. Their buildings were aligned with the risings of the moon and sun at key seasons. On the nearby Fajada Butte were symbols of the cosmos carved into the rock in just the right spot so that daggers of light shone through the heart of these drawings on the winter and summer solstice, as well as both equinoxes.

So it is likely on that morning over a thousand years ago there were people looking up in the sky to see an amazing event — the appearance of a supernova in the constellation we know as Taurus.

In our time that supernova is now identified with the object known as the Crab Nebula. It blew up with tremendous force 5,000 years ago and its light still took 4,000 years to get here. Scientists estimate that if it had been less than fifty light years from our planet all life would have been destroyed.

This new star so bright that it appeared not as a twinkling dot but as a many-rayed object. Moreover, when the sun arose shortly thereafter the new star did not disappear. It was visible in the night sky for nearly two years.

Many believe that the pictograph at Chaco Canyon commemorates that supernova. There are other pictographs throughout the southwest that seem to show the crescent moon and a bright star together. It was only in the American Southwest that the supernova appeared next to the crescent moon when it burst into the sky.

The Anasazi were not the only ones to observe this wonder. Chinese and Japanese astronomers also saw the star and wrote down precisely when it first appeared and when it finally faded from view 653 days later.

We do not know with what wonder and awe the Anasazi viewed the star, though it was significant enough to commemorate.

What is known is that evidently it was not noticed or seen by Europeans, who did not leave behind any records of this wonderful event. A great light shone, and it was all for nothing in Christendom. It shone for nothing.

What is the use of a great light that shines upon the people living in darkness if no one takes notice of it? What is the point if its wonder does not touch our hearts, nor directs our thoughts beyond ourselves to something greater?

Epiphany 4 / Ordinary Time 4
Matthew 5:1-12
by John Sumwalt

Mercy, Mercy

Blessed are the merciful, for they shall receive mercy.
— Matthew 5:7

There was once a little girl named Mercy. Isn't that an unusual name? Mercy didn't think it was unusual, because it had always been her name and seemed perfectly normal to her. In fact, her mom had told her that it was a very special name, which means to show kindness to someone in need or to forgive someone who has wronged you, even though they don't deserve to be forgiven.

One day, Mercy and some of her friends were playing tag in the backyard when a baby robin fell from somewhere overhead and hit the ground in front of them with a loud plop. When they looked up, they could see that it had fallen out of a nest in a large oak tree which stood on the edge of Mercy's yard. One of the children picked up the dazed bird and threw it into the air to see if it could fly. But the poor bird was too young to fly, and it hit the ground again with a thud. "Oh, be careful," Mercy said. "We mustn't hurt it. We must put it back in the nest so its mother can take care of it until it learns how to fly."

Very gently, so as not to harm it, Mercy picked up the little bird. She tucked it into the soft corner of her pocket, carefully climbed up into the oak tree, and placed it back into the nest with its brothers and sisters. The little bird seemed glad to be home.

Mercy felt very good about what she had done. But as she was thinking about how proud her mother would be when she told her about it, something terrible happened. She slipped as she was climbing down and fell out of the tree, right on top of one of her neighbor's prize-winning rosebushes. She didn't fall far, so she wasn't badly hurt; just a scratch and a couple of bruises. But the rosebush was smashed, and Mercy knew it was her neighbor's favorite.

When Mercy looked up, her neighbor, Mrs. Black, was standing over her, looking down at the broken rosebush. She had been watching from the window. Mercy was scared. She was certain that Mrs. Black was going to yell at her, and worse yet, probably tell her mother. Then she wouldn't be allowed to play with her friends for a week.

Mrs. Black helped Mercy up off the rosebush. It was broken near the base, and there was no hope at all that it could be saved. Mercy waited for the worst. Mrs. Black said, "Mercy, I saw what you did. It was very good of you to help that poor little bird. It was a kind and merciful thing to do. It's too bad about the rosebush. I know you didn't mean to break it, so I'm not going to say anything to your mother. But the next time you need to climb a tree, please remember to ask a grown-up to help you."

Mercy was very happy that she wasn't going to be punished. And she never forgot, for as long as she lived, how Mrs. Black had shown her mercy.

Epiphany 5 / Ordinary Time 5
Isaiah 58:1-9a (9b-12)
by Peter Andrew Smith

The Way to God

Once there were a people who built themselves a great nation. They established a land of law, opportunity, and peace. They enjoyed the good things of life as they unravelled the mysteries of the natural world and banished afflictions that their ancestors had faced.

Yet despite all their prosperity and accomplishments the people were still restless and unfulfilled. There was something missing. After a time of searching and wondering, they realized that in establishing their challenging yet comfortable lives, in their quest to know and comprehend, they had moved away from God.

"How do we return to God?" they asked each other. Through contemplation and careful consideration, they decided there were things that they needed to do in order to become spiritual people. They went about filling the void in their lives with great enthusiasm and energy.

Magnificent places of worship were designed and built, sacred writings were analysed and dissected for meaning, and spiritual activities became part of their everyday lives. They became quite proud of their great churches and loved to spout the wisdom that they read in books and made great productions of prayer and fasting. The best among them memorized and recited long prayers and the most devoted would publicly fast to show their piety.

Yet they came no closer to knowing or understanding God. No matter how much they worked and fasted, no matter how much they tried to be holy the restlessness and unfulfilled part within them remained. They were no closer to God.

"There must not be a God," some decided and they turned away from all things spiritual.

"We must not be doing enough," others concluded and redoubled their efforts to be holy.

Yet despite their efforts, both these groups were unhappy. Those who renounced spiritual things still found life empty, and those who tried to do more things to be spiritual discovered nothing satisfying no matter how hard they tried.

There were some among the people who knew there was a God and felt that they were doing something wrong. They began to believe that there was a key thing they were missing, some element that they were not understanding, something that they needed to connect with God.

"God," they wondered aloud. "What are we doing wrong?"

God led them to neighbours who were hungry and whispered "Fast." The people fed the hungry even as they denied themselves worldly things and began to understand more the plight of those around them.

God showed them the injustices that existed even in their wonderful nation and whispered "Pray." The people prayed to know God's will and God's way and caught an idea on how to live out the kingdom of heaven here on earth. That vision motivated their work and efforts.

God set before them stories of faith and wisdom, the sacred writings of God's people, and whispered "Listen." The people quieted their busy lives, their work and activity. They considered what God had to say to them and committed themselves to growing in God's way.

They served as they worshiped, they learned as they taught, and they discovered that the way of faith was difficult, the path was not always certain, the struggles were sometimes tiring. Yet through all of those times they realized that God was with them even as they were with each other and the world. For they came to understand that to be people of faith it is not enough to want to come to God, you also need to let God come to you.

Epiphany 6 / Ordinary Time 6
Deuteronomy 30:15-20
by C. David McKirachan

Choose Life

I was offered crisis intervention and suicide prevention as a course in seminary. It went into a good amount of theory but it was a nuts and bolts course that developed an awareness of the dos and don'ts in dealing with an individual in crisis and how to effectively intervene. We also learned about the dark night of suicide. We also learned how to determine the level of lethality from which the person spoke. This analytical instrument had been developed by studying individuals who had committed suicide and looking at the most common elements in their lives.

During this study it became clear that commonalities were not sophisticated dynamics, but simple lifestyle issues that in combination created a lethal pattern in the individual. Simple things like health, not serious illness, but any kind of sickness including the common cold could make a person more vulnerable. Did the person have access to a friend, a person who they could count on to listen to them, to care about them? Did the person have a stable place to live or was their environment chaotic?

It occurred to me that an awful lot of the religious rules or laws that we teach and preach about and offer as guides for people were down to earth practical guidelines for living. Just about that time the teacher offered this passage, "See, I have set before you this day life and good, death and evil." The teacher warned us not to try to use religion in trying to help the tortured souls that were teetering on the knife edge of life and death. Religion may have been part of what had isolated and hurt them. But he went on to say faith that is worth anything, faith that can in any way be called good news offers empathy rather than judgment and more the possibility for a person to make a choice for a life that can flourish, even in difficult circumstances.

I learned a lot in that course. I ended up on a suicide hotline for two years. The lessons went beyond my participation in that experience. I learned that we tend to get in the way of the rules of life. In our rush to solve people's issues, we forget that life is a gift of God and that the simple capability that rests in each of us can do wonders. Our job as helpers is to allow the person to access their own capability to choose life, even abundant life.

I also came in contact with people who lost their way, for whom the balance tipped toward darkness. It was sad, frightening, and forced me to deliberately hold on to the rules of life, the good news that I claimed as the core of my life. There, in those moments we were encouraged to stay close to each other, to reach out and touch each other. I discovered the importance of honesty and intimacy in building a healthy life.

Somebody said something about that once, "Love one another as I have loved you." Good rule for life.

Epiphany 7 / Ordinary Time 7
1 Corinthians 3:10-11, 16-23
by John Sumwalt

What Kind of Fool Are You?

If you think that you are wise in this age, you should become fools so that you may become wise. For the wisdom of this world is foolishness with God.
— 1 Corinthians 3:18-19

There are many different kinds of fools. When I preach the apostle Paul's words about fools and foolishness in 1 Corinthians, I begin the sermon with two of my favorite Abraham Lincoln stories:

In her book, *Yankee From Olympus*, Catherine Drinker Bowen describes the day President Lincoln visited Fort Stevens not far from Washington DC. "It was July 12, 1864... The president climbed a parapet. He had never seen a battle... The firing began... On the parapet five feet from him a man fell. Three feet away, so close Lincoln could have touched him, an officer fell dead. 'Get down, you fool!' a young voice shouted. Automatically the president stepped back. It was Wendell Holmes, angry and terrified. From the protection of the bulwark, Lincoln looked down at the white face, streaked with dirt... 'Captain,' he said, 'I'm glad you know how to talk to a civilian.' "

In 1902, Oliver Wendell Holmes Jr. was appointed by President Theodore Roosevelt to serve as an Associate Justice of the Supreme Court, where he served in distinction for thirty years, retiring in 1932, at the age of ninety.

Pat Hickey summarized another favorite Lincoln story in an article in the March 3rd issue of the *Washington Times*.

He describes what was to be a duel to the death, a fool's act that Lincoln would regret for the rest of his life:

"The duel between Abraham Lincoln and Illinois State Auditor James J. Shields was to take place by the Mississippi River near Alton, Illinois, on September 22, 1842. Earlier, there had appeared in the *Sangamo* journal, a Whig newspaper based in the state capital of Springfield, a series of letters attacking Shields under the *nom de plume* "Rebecca." Shields' honesty, courage, integrity, and national origin were treated with abuse and sharp wit...."

Many historians have concluded that the future president collaborated with his future wife, Mary Todd, and Julia Jayne, a friend, on the letters. "Shields confronted Lincoln. Though illegal in Illinois, the challenge gained momentum, and the newspapers of the time publicized the event for weeks. It would have been difficult for any man, let alone a politician on the rise, to back down. As the individual challenged, Lincoln had the choice of weapons and chose large cavalry broadswords. While seconds argued the protocols, cooler heads attempted to prevail. Shields would not be mollified, however. At one point, looking to deter Shields, the 6-foot-4-inch Lincoln reached with his broadsword and cut a length of branch from a tree, showing Shields how his seven-inch height advantage gave him an edge. Eventually, bloodshed was avoided, and Lincoln apologized. Lincoln and Shields ultimately became friends."

Carl Sandburg wrote in his biography, *Lincoln: The Prairie Years and The War Years*, that "the duel had become a joke but Lincoln never afterward mentioned it and his friends saw it as a sore point that shouldn't be spoken of to him. A story arose and lived on that when first, as the challenged party, he had his choice of weapons, he said, 'How about cow dung at five paces?' " (New York: Harcourt, Brace & World, Inc, 1954, p. 77)

Hickey added that later, "During the Civil War, an officer asked the president about the aborted duel, and an angry Lincoln advised him to never speak of it again."

I will conclude the sermon with brief accounts of two well-known martyrs who lived and died for the foolishness of the gospel by giving their lives for others as Christ did.

Oscar Romero, assassinated as he celebrated Mass, was Archbishop in El Salvador during the late 1970s and spoke out passionately for the poor and against the violence of government soldiers that became known as death squads.

Peter Feuerherd wrote of Archbishop Romero in the December 2010 edition of *St. Anthony Messenger* magazine:

> At a time when the press in El Salvador was heavily censored, his Sunday homilies, broadcast over the radio, offered hope for those who wanted recognition and condemnation of massacres in the countryside, as government troops and militias swept through whole villages, killing thousands. Romero heard the stories as he listened to peasants who trekked... to their archbishop's office, pleading with him to say something. So he did. Romero's condemnations of the violence became bolder toward the end of his three-year tenure as archbishop. He challenged wealthy Catholic families, who were well-known for public displays of piety but financed death squads. He emphasized the church's call for the rights of workers to organize, and decried the poverty that caused so many Salvadorans to leave the country in search of work. He called upon the leaders of the only country formally dedicated to Jesus, the Savior, to live up to its namesake.

On March 23, 1980, Archbishop Romero made the following appeal to the men of the armed forces:

> Brothers, you came from our own people. You are killing your own brothers. Any human order to kill must be subordinate to the law of God, which says, "Thou shalt not kill." No soldier is obliged to obey an order

> contrary to the law of God. No one has to obey an immoral law. It is high time you obeyed your consciences rather than sinful orders. The church cannot remain silent before such an abomination.... In the name of God, in the name of this suffering people whose cry rises to heaven more loudly each day, I implore you, I beg you, I order you: stop the repression.

Archbishop Romero was murdered the day after this speech was heard on the radio.

The story of Maximilian Kolbe, a Polish friar, who took the place of another man who was sentenced to die at Auschwitz, is told by Chuck Colson in *The Volunteer at Auschwitz*. Colson describes the scene in the death camp:

> A prisoner from Barracks 14, where Father Kolbe was housed, managed to escape. The prisoners from that barracks were paraded before the commandant... a monster named Fritsch, levied sentence. "Ten of you will die in the starvation bunker." The starvation bunker was the horror of horrors: both food and water were denied; many prisoners spent their dying days howling, attacking each other, clawing the walls in a frenzy of fear....
>
> Fritsch walked down the lines of prisoners, selecting his victims. One poor wretch, whose number — 5659 — was on the list, groaned and cried out: "My poor wife, my poor children, what will they do?" Suddenly, there was a commotion in the ranks. A prisoner had broken out of line, calling for the commandant....
>
> "Halt!" he called. "What does this Polish pig want of me?" The prisoners gasped... It was Father Kolbe who had spoken... The frail priest spoke softly to the Nazi butcher. "I would like to die in place of one of the men you condemned."
>
> "Why?" shouted the commandant. The priest bowed his head: "I am an old man, sir, and good for nothing."
>
> "In whose place do you want to die?"

> "For that one," Kolbe responded, pointing to the weeping prisoner — number 5659 — who had cried for his wife and children. "Who are you?" asked Fritsch. The prisoner looked back at him, a strange fire in his dark eyes. "I am a priest." "Ein Pfaffe!" the commandant snorted. He nodded to his assistant. Number 5659 was crossed out, and number 16670 — Kolbe's number — replaced it. Father Kolbe died as he had lived, serving and loving others. From the death cell came not the sounds of frenzied despair but the faint sounds of singing. This time, the prisoners had a shepherd to lead them through the shadows of the valley of death.
> (story adapted from Chuck Colson, "The Volunteer at Auschwitz,?" in *The Book of Virtues*, William J. Bennett, ed. [New York: Simon and Schuster, 1993], pp. 806-807)

Before his death, Maximillian Kolbe wrote to a fellow priest:

> It is sad to see how in our times the disease called "indifferentism" is spreading in all its forms, not just among those in the world but also among the members of religious orders. But indeed, since God is worthy of infinite glory, it is our first and most pressing duty to give him such glory as we, in our weakness, can manage — even that we would never, poor exiled creatures that we are, be able to render him such glory as he truly deserves. Because God's glory shines through most brightly in the salvation of the souls that Christ redeemed with his own blood, let it be the chief concern of the apostolic life to bring salvation and an increase in holiness to as many souls as possible.

As I said, "There are many different kinds of fools." What kind of fool are you?

Transfiguration of Our Lord
(Last Sunday after Epiphany)
Matthew 17:1-9
by C. David McKirachan

Jesus Was an Alien!

I went to seminary in Berkeley, California. The town is affectionately known as Bezerk-ley. Taking that into account you'd expect lots of crazy stuff to come up. I did. I looked forward to it. I instigated some of it. So, one day we were dealing with the Transfiguration and one of my fellow students, with the excitement of a true believer, began the class saying he had found conclusive proof in this passage for Jesus being an alien. It had to do with the cloud and the brilliance with which Jesus shone. The word in Greek had more to do with dazzling reflection from metal than with bright cloth. They saw a spaceship, and Jesus went up there to meet the pilots, Moses and Elijah.

Poo-poo it we may, from our high positions of theologically esoteric heights or geographical prejudice, but the space ship scenario makes more sense according to our materialistic understanding of everything than some spiritual visitation of prophets to the man Jesus as he prepared to journey into the mouth of the beast. This is nuts. It's almost as nuts as angels appearing to unwed mothers and shepherds, let alone Iranian NSA agents. But that's another story. This is okay for biblical epics, but really, how can self-respecting highly educated, thinking human beings buy this stuff?

The judgment here is on our buying into the barren mythology of our culture. The logic of the story is firm. Jesus revealed himself to be at home with giants of the faith, people whose relationship with God was as intimate as any had ever been. They were people who served the Lord and struggled with doubt and trouble and loneliness. And they came to this one who was facing a task that had never been demanded of any of God's children. It also places Jesus teaching about the kingdom of God in another light, a dazzling light, if you will. Jesus may have been a man, but he came from someplace west of California, and I don't mean Hawaii. In this passage we see Jesus at home with souls that he knew.

Now I don't even pretend to understand what the above means. But maybe that's the point. Maybe this intersection is there to remind us that there are things going on here that are beyond our understanding, and that's not a bad thing. Maybe this reminds us not to sell this Jesus guy short. But in spite of all the dazzling and clouding and special effect action, Jesus brought these guys, his three disciples up there to be with him. Maybe we are also to remember that we, limited, fearful beings are just as important to him as Moses and Elijah. Maybe this earth is just as important to God as heaven. Maybe we're so good at forgetting that that we need to be dazzled once in a while. And we need to be invited to come down off the cloudy mountains of revelation to another, smaller hill with three crosses on it.

Now you want to hear a crazy story? Meet me at the other end of Lent.

Ash Wednesday
Joel 2:1-2, 12-17
by Peter Andrew Smith

The Terrible Dark Day

Carried by the wind, a small pod covered with spikes fell onto a field. The precious seeds within spilled into the ground and after the rains fell, one of them sprouted and took root. A tiny shoot pushed up through the ground and reached toward the light. The shoot grew into a sapling, which grew into a small tree.

As the tree's branches spread out, a bird flying past landed and took rest among its leaves. The bird flew on but soon other birds used the branches of the young tree as a resting place. One bird took shelter there from the elements and returned time and time again to the tree. As the tree grew larger the bird built a nest, attracted a mate, and soon the nest was filled with eggs. The eggs hatched and the baby birds used the branches of the tree as places to sing their songs and build their own nests.

As the seasons passed, the tree kept reaching toward the sun. The branches grew thicker and the trunk grew sturdy and strong. In the middle of the field, the tree stood tall and proud anchored firmly by deep roots that tightly gripped the earth.

When the time came, tiny pods covered with spikes containing precious seeds appeared on the branches of the tree. They started small, then grew, and when it was their time, they fell upon the ground. Each one of those pods landed under the shadow of the mighty tree with its full branches and towering height. Without the light of the sun and the kiss of the rain, the seeds never took root and simply rotted where they fell.

One season the tree stopped reaching for the sun. The branches did not extend any further and the roots did not seek any deeper. The birds that were there remained but no new ones came to the tree or near the field where the lone tree stood tall and full. The leaves still came each spring and fell each autumn. When it was time, the pods full of precious seeds developed and dropped from the tree but the seeds never went beyond the shadow of the tree and none of them ever sprouted.

The insects came seeking to eat away at the vitality of the tree as did the various diseases that sought to overcome its health. Each time the great branches, sturdy trunk, and the deep roots allowed the tree to resist. Yet, each time the tree took longer to heal itself following the assault of the forces looking to consume its life.

One season when the spiky pods had again sprouted on the tree, the sky grew dark during the day. As the light died, the birds stopped their songs, and huddled close to the trunk of the tree as an eerie silence covered the field. The calm was broken by the gentle rustle of the leaves. The gentle rustle grew to a roar as a persistent wind began to blow. The leaves shook and the birds hung on in the shelter of the many branches of the great tall tree. The persistent wind became a raging gale. Nests were pulled apart and scattered to the wind as eggs smashed into the ground and the birds were driven from their refuge.

The wind tore and bit into the tree pulling and tearing at it. Leaves were ripped in pieces and torn from the branches. The branches themselves strained under the fury of the wind. The smallest ones were twisted back and forth until they snapped off. The larger ones bent and strained under the relentless pressure.

The wind crashed and pounded against the tree with such a terrible fury that the mighty trunk itself began to sway from side to side. The roots struggled to hold the tree in place as the wind slammed into the tree again and again. Then all at once the wind stopped.

The once-mighty tree stood broken and battered among the shattered nests and debris. The roots had only a fragile hold on the earth and sap dripped from cracks in the trunk. The branches hung twisted and warped, stripped bare of all but a leaf here and there. Only the memory of the tree's former majesty remained as the light returned and a gentle rain began to fall.

As the days passed, the tree began to grow new leaves and the branches spread out in the embrace of the light. The roots tightened their grip on the earth and then dug deeper into the ground. New branches grew in place of those which had been lost and the tree reached upward once again. The birds slowly returned to the branches. Nests and songs of life returned to the tree.

Beyond where the branches stretched, pods covered in spikes broke open and the seeds within fell into the embrace of the earth. The seeds took root and grew into saplings. The saplings pushed toward the light and as their branches reached out they grew strong and tall outside the shadow of the tree that had stood for so long by itself in the field. After the terrible dark day, the tree was no longer alone in the field. It stood in the middle of a new forest.

Lent 1
Genesis 2:15-17; 3:1-7
by C. David McKirachan

It's Not My Fault

Through the years one of the most frustrating exchanges I've had with my sons has always gone something like, "This room is wrecked" (that's me), "I didn't do it" (that is one of them). "Well, let's clean it up" (that's me), "I didn't make the mess, why should I have to clean it up?" (that's one of them). "I don't care who made the mess, it's got to get cleaned up" (that's an irate me). "That's not fair" (that is the philosophically whining them). "Right. Such is life" (that is the existentialist me). I kept waiting for them to grow into seeing and doing, into taking responsibility for having a nice living space. What they gave me on a consistent basis was an argument about whose fault the situation was.

They're not alone. Our justice system is big on measuring culpability. Our civil legal system is big on assigning blame. Our political system uses scapegoats to avoid responsibility and divert attention. Corporations are big at blame. Don't forget your paper trail. And then there's marriage and divorce. Almost never do we face a situation with the attitude, "Here's the mess we have — now let's get to it."

I think the biblical story of the fall demonstrates this so well. We're so ready to blame the snake. He just happens to be crafty. I think he does pretty well for a reptile with a weird tongue. No lisp recorded in my Bible. Then we blame Eve. I've heard so many jokes about Eve, most of them sexist. How would you like to be the mother of humanity? Talk about a setup. You'd be guilty for everything. Then there's

Adam. Here come the cracks and jokes again. Good old Dad. Can't get no respect.

Sin belongs to all of us. It doesn't matter who did the deed. We've got to live with the mess and do our best to clean it up — unless we want to remain children and continue driving our parent nuts. Okay, now we're down to it. It's hard to let go of the child thing. It feels like we're sheltered when we can argue with the parents, because it reminds us of the time when we weren't responsible for soup to nuts — the time when there was somebody in charge who could make sense of the whole thing.

The hardest part of losing my parents, other than missing them, was realizing that now I was an adult. Now, whether I whined or not, I was in charge of making things happen. No safety net. I think God wants us to grow up. When it comes down to it, it doesn't really matter whose fault it happens to be — we've still got the mess to clean up. Our brothers and sisters are in trouble and no matter how good or pure or wise we happen to be, it's all in the family.

Maybe we were thrown out of the garden because we became adolescents. Even God would have a hard time with a sixteen-year-old.

Lent 2
John 3:1-17
by John Smylie

Three Field Goals and a Touchdown

There were only two minutes left in the game. The home team called a timeout — they were behind by 16 points, but at this point it was a matter of pride. They knew they had very little chance of winning — they had been outplayed through most of the game but still they were fighting to score so as not to be shut out. The other team had already scored three field goals and a touchdown and an extra point. The team was not comfortable with 16-0 — they wanted to get something on the board.

"Come on boys," the coach said as his voice broke huddle on the sidelines as the boys prepared to walk back on to the field, "Let's not get shut out." It was evening, the sun was already below the horizon, and the last glimmers of sunshine tickled the clouds with pink light. The crowd was cheering the boys on, the band was beating on their drums from the sideline, the cheerleaders were shaking their pom-poms, and the boys went out onto the field. They were already on the opposing team's 30-yard line with two minutes left in the game. Their field-goal kicker had a range of about 40 yards and so the boys needed to move the ball at least seven more yards.

The boys lined up in a passing formation, the ball was hiked, and the quarterback pretended to throw the ball out to the right side of the field to his wide receiver and then tucked the ball under his arm and ran straight ahead. There was a slight hole in the middle of the line and he picked up four yards. Second down, another run, and three more yards and only 45 seconds left on the clock. Third down brought a quarterback sneak moving the ball a bit closer to the center of the field, one more yard gained. Fourth down, six seconds left on the clock, and the last time out used. The ball was now on the 22-yard line and when you add ten yards for the end zone and seven yards for the snap, the kicker was facing a 39-yard field goal right at the edge of his range.

In the stands there was a fan who had been holding up a sign all game long. The sign read — 3:16. Now the kicker, his name was Fred, was a member of an organization that involved Christian athletes and he knew what 3:16 meant. "For God so loved the world that he gave his only son, so that everyone who believes in him may not perish but may have eternal life." The kicker smiled to himself thinking that he had an opportunity to make the score 3-16.

It was fourth down, the ball on the 22-yard line, the snap was good — the hold was good — the kick was good — 3-16 was the final score. The crowd erupted even though their team had lost — the band played the school fight song — the cheerleaders screamed — the players held their heads a little higher as they greeted the opposing team.

It was quiet in the locker room as the boys showered and changed into their civilian clothes. The coach commended the boys on their final effort and said that he would see them on Monday when they came to practice. One of the boys whose name was Joe came up to the kicker and asked, "Did you see that guy in the stands holding a sign that said 3:16?"

"Yeah, I did. In fact when I saw it, it gave me some courage and confidence as I was getting ready to kick the ball."

"What do you mean? I thought the guy was kind of a nut, but now I wonder if he was some sort of prophet. How did he know the score would be 3-16?"

The kicker smiled and wondered if this might be the deeper reason for the score being what it was. His teammate who was asking him about the gentleman in the stands and his 3:16 sign was a young man with a deeply troubled past. He'd been in one foster home after another. His parents had been drug addicts, caught up in the methamphetamine addiction pattern. It was amazing that he was doing as well as he was, but there was a very hard edge to him and he'd never been exposed to the gospel.

Fred the kicker said, "Let me tell you about that guy who was holding a sign, let me tell you where he got that score from. I'm heading over to a meeting now for the Fellowship of Christian athletes, why don't you come with me and I'll explain it to you."

"Sure, why not, I've got nothing else to do, sounds good," said Joe.

The boys got into a 1962 VW bug and headed over to the back of a coffee shop where the meeting was held. On the way, Fred explained to Joe what John 3:16 was. He described why it was so important to so many — and why he figured the man in the stands was holding up a placard with those numbers in bold print. Then he explained how that verse fit into the whole story. He told Joe how there was a rather well-known man named Nicodemus who was a leader among his people who came to Jesus by night. That was a big risk, Fred told Joe, because if Nicodemus had been seen by his own people he would have likely been rejected — seen as some sort of traitor to his faith.

Fred went on to tell Joe that it seemed like lots of folks even today were afraid to find out about Jesus. "You know Joe, you and I are kind of like Nicodemus tonight, we're going to a meeting in the back of a coffee shop, most everybody else on our team will be going out to parties, but you and I — well maybe we'll learn something tonight that will have real value for us for the rest of our lives. I'm kind of glad the score was 3-16. It's given me an opportunity to do something that I'm usually too chicken to do. Joe I'm not sure anybody on the team knows that I come to these Fellowship of Christian athletes meetings, but I'm glad you know and I hope you find what I find in them."

"Joe," Fred said, "I've usually been too embarrassed to invite anybody to the meetings, especially my teammates. I find myself nervous that I will be rejected by the team — you know we kickers often feel like we are on the edge of the whole team experience as it is — and so while the team goes off and does its thing I tend to gravitate to my church and small group — Joe thanks for coming with me tonight."

Joe was not used to being talked to this way. There was a deep hunger in him to be included somewhere, to be a part of something greater than himself. That was a big part of the reason of why he was on the football team, he wanted to be part of a group, part of something greater than himself, but he was disappointed that he hardly ever got to play. "Fred, I'd like to learn more about Nicodemus and I'm glad the score was 3-16, thanks for inviting me to the meeting tonight."

They drove in silence for a while and Fred thought to himself — I'm glad they made three field goals and a touchdown — and I sure am glad I made that kick at the end of the game. He marveled a bit at how these things came together because he had wanted to invite someone to join him at the Fellowship of Christian athletes for a while. Perhaps more than ever before he believed that God really did love the world, and God cared about him and Joe and that God would do anything to open the door to lead them to eternal life. He was glad for the journey that Nicodemus made those many years ago and he was glad for their own journey. All because of three field goals, a touchdown, and a 39-yard field goal with time expiring at the end of the game, there was rejoicing in heaven as well as on the sidelines and in the coffee shop!

Lent 3
Romans 5:1-11
by Keith Hewitt

The Account

"Will there be anything else?" the shopkeeper asked, as he finished wrapping the meat in white paper, then tied it tightly with white string that came from a spool that hung just overhead, above the top of the cooler.

The woman looked at the groceries gathered there — flour, check; eggs, check; sausage, check; ground beef, check — then glanced at her list, mentally scratched off a couple of items that were just too expensive; she had included them on a whim, hoping that they might be on sale at the little corner market. Jago sometimes did that, if he could catch something that was about to turn, but hadn't quite gone bad, yet. She shook her head. "That's it, thanks." Pause. "Can you put this on our account, please?"

"Sure thing," the man answered, almost at once. He wrote up a receipt, showed it to her, then stuck it on a spindle next to the cash register, along with a couple of dozen others. Later, he would go into his books and add the day's groceries to the tab they had running; she looked away, shocked once at how much she had spent, and again at how much she thought would be available to spend.

"Walter gets paid tomorrow, doesn't he?" the shopkeeper asked as he packed the groceries into a plain brown bag. He almost managed to sound casual.

She appeared to think for a moment, then nodded slightly. "Yes, yes he does. I'm surprised you remember."

He shrugged, rubbed a finger under his eye, bumping up his glasses. "You kind of have to these days. You've got to know who's not working, and who is — and when they get paid. You know —" He hesitated, then smiled shyly. "My wife gets nervous about all these accounts, and when they're going to get paid." He shrugged again, bumped his glasses, "I tell her, 'Don't worry so much, it's not good for you. Besides, now that Roosevelt is in, things are going to get better.'"

"I sure hope so," she said, and reached for the bag. "Thanks for your help — and your understanding."

He held the bag for the barest moment as she started to take it and looked at her through thick lenses that made his eyes seem huge. "We need to have something paid on your account," he said quietly, almost apologetically. "It's up past forty dollars, now."

She nodded again, sliding the bag across the counter, turning her eyes away. "Of course," she said. "Tomorrow, then." She cradled the bag in her arms and walked out the door, listened to the jingling bell that mocked her with its airy cheeriness as she pulled the door open. She walked down the couple of concrete steps to the sidewalk, rounded the corner, and hurried home, feet taking her on her way while her mind struggled with other things. $40? It had to be closer to $45, she calculated, trying to remember her last couple of purchases.

When was the last time they'd been able to pay down the account? She shook her head; the longer they went, the worse it got. They lived at the mercy of her husband's job, and there just hadn't been that many hours lately. He was a die maker, a good, solid job that a man ought to be able to raise a family on — but when the factory sat idle, there was no need for his skills.

She fretted about it the rest of the night — as she had so many other nights before — in silence that sat like a rock on her chest. She couldn't talk to him about it — he had other worries — and there was no talking to the children, of course. Although they must suspect — they must all suspect something, she thought. How thin could you make a stew, before it became soup — and how thin could you make the soup, before it became broth? But nobody ever said anything, sitting around the table.

She was waiting for her husband the next day when he came home from work. As he did each payday, he went to the Building & Loan to cash his check, and pay on their mortgage, returning with whatever was left over tucked away in a creased white envelope. It had been a better week than others she thought as he took the envelope out of his pocket — they ought to be able to knock some of the forty-plus dollars down. She thought about what they would do, what they could pay off, what they should keep for expenses....

Across the table, their daughters ate butter and sugar sandwiches, watching as the ritual played out.

He put his thumb under the flap, ripped it down the length of the envelope, and puffed it open, dumped out the contents on the pale yellow linoleum tablecloth. The bill slid out silently, the coins clinked softly, almost drowned out by the noise of the wind in the leaves outside the kitchen window. She stared at what was left of his pay, even as he lowered his head and turned away. Her fingers flashed out to the table, shaking slightly as she sorted through once, then again, to be sure. The answer was the same both times: $1.27.

The hope that had stirred for a moment — even as a part of her knew it was fantasy — sank, and sucked her soul down with it, a torpedoed ship that took dreams to the bottom where they would never see the light of day again. After what seemed like a long time, she realized the girls were still there — she looked at them, forced a smile, and said gently, "It's good. There's something left over this week."

And hated the lie.

Although Columbus Street ran along the crest of a hill, when she walked to the market after dinner it seemed like a steep, uphill journey. For a block, she spun possibilities in her mind, tops of flashing ideas that whirled and wobbled, then crashed on the hard floor of reality. She turned the corner in front of the market, stopped and looked in the window for a moment or two; there was nobody else in there. She mounted the steps, pulled open the door, and listened to the bell announce her presence.

The store smelled of fresh meat and despair, the floorboards beneath her creaked as she walked directly to the counter at the back of the store. Jago was there, sorting through the receipts on the spindle next to the cash register, transferring charges into an open ledger. He looked up and seemed surprised to see her. "Hello," he said, capping the fountain pen in his hand and closing the big book. "I wasn't expecting to see you again, so soon."

"I said I would be here," she reminded him. "Remember, Walter got paid today."

"I know, but —" he opened the ledger, ran a finger down the side of the page, as though to check something, then looked up again. "— I assumed you knew."

"Knew what?"

He put a hand over the names above hers, turned the book around so she could see it. "Your account — it was paid off this morning. A gentleman came in and asked about it, but it seemed like he already knew what the tab was. And then he paid it." He stabbed a fingertip at the balance column. "See: zero balance. You're paid in full."

Her heart was racing, wanted to fly out of her chest. "Who — who —?" she repeated, stumbling, unable to complete the thought.

"I don't know." He shrugged, bumped his glasses with his finger. "He seemed like a nice young man but never gave his name. He just said maybe you would find him some day — if you wanted to look for him." He closed the book again and peered at her with out-sized eyes. "Did you need anything else tonight?"

"No." She shook her head. "No, we're fine. Thank you." She retreated quickly from the store, afraid to linger, lest he discover it was some kind of mistake. As she walked home, steps clicking fast and loud on the sidewalk, she tried to imagine who could have done it, or what might have happened. As she pondered the mystery and the wonder of what seemed like being born again, she noticed something else: Although Columbus Street was level, the way home seemed downhill.

To fully understand the beauty of sunlight, you must spend some time in the dark. To fully understand — and appreciate — the gifts of hope and forgiveness that Jesus shares with us, we must understand how truly desperate and hopeless our situations are without them. We each owe a debt that we can't possibly pay, ourselves — but if we will just open our hearts to him, offer ourselves to him, believe in the gift that he offers, Jesus will be there to pay it off for us.

Lent 4
John 9:1-41
by Peter Andrew Smith

The Disturbing Witness of Grace

"Why?" Susan asked.

Everyone tensed around the table and no one met her gaze. People shifted uncomfortably in their seats as her question echoed in the room.

"We are not going to reconsider our decision," the chairperson said as he adjusted his glasses.

"I'm aware of that," Susan said. "I simply want to know why you do not want to hire me, since I have the degree, experience, and am willing to accept what you are able to pay."

"You are not a suitable person to be our youth minister," the chairperson said. "Our decision is final."

"Yes," she said trying to keep her voice calm. "I understand that. I even grudgingly accept that. But what I do not understand is why you think I am unacceptable to teach young people."

"We don't have to give an explanation," he repeated.

"Since you called me to come to this second interview I think you owe me an explanation," she said.

The shifting of the committee members in their chairs increased and they continued to look away from her.

"We discovered after you were invited to this meeting that you do not have suitable character," the chairperson said. "Let us leave it at that."

"That isn't good enough. My references are impeccable, my previous work experience is...."

The chairperson slammed his pen onto the desk. "You made those movies. There is no way that we are going to let someone who did such degenerate things teach about Jesus and his love to our young people."

Susan looked down. "I did some things that I am not proud of when I was younger." She looked up. "That was before I came to know Jesus in my life."

"That doesn't matter," he said. "A youth minister is supposed to be a role model, the children are going to look up to you. You have to have impeccable character."

Everyone around the room murmured in agreement.

"I agree completely," Susan said. "Any minister of the church should live the message of Jesus in their life. I did not know about God's love for me when I did those things. I thank God that one night I wandered into a church during a service and heard the preacher tell about forgiveness and grace. I cried that whole night when I realized that I didn't have to live the way I was living. I changed that day. By God's love and through God's grace I left the life I had been in and I have never looked back."

She took a deep breath. "Eventually I realized that God was calling me to work with young people as a minister and I studied, worked, and served the church in that way. As you can see I have been in a number of churches setting up successful youth programs and Sunday schools —"

"None of that matters," the chairperson said waving his hands. "We are not hiring you. You do not have suitable character to work with children. If they ever learned that you had made those movies...."

"Or actually saw clips from one of them," one of the women piped in.

"Exactly!" the chairperson said. "We would lose all credibility as a church."

"I don't advertise my past indiscretions. But in the internet age no sin like mine stays hidden long." Susan looked the chairperson in the eyes. "It came up at the last church I worked at as a youth minister. Some teenage girls asked me. I was honest about what I did and told the teens the truth about how it demeans and diminishes what God intends for us and our bodies. I was firm that the path I was on at their age is filled with lies, hurt, and harm both physical and spiritual. I also told them that I know God can forgive anything and everything through Jesus and offers us a fresh chance to live differently."

"And is that why you are looking for a new church? Because people found out?"

Susan shook her head. "I spoke to the church board the day after I spoke to the teens. With the blessing of the church board, I worked another five years at that church. I'm here because my husband took a transfer to this city."

The chairperson scowled. "I cannot comment about the irresponsible actions of the churches you were at before. But hearing your story means nothing to me. All I know is that we have no place for a sinner like you among us."

A murmur of agreement echoed in the room from the other committee members.

"I'm sorry that my story doesn't make a difference to you," Susan said as she picked up her papers to leave. "I'll pray that one day it will matter to you because I don't know how you can be a church without knowing grace and the one who gives it."

Lent 5
Ezekiel 37:1-14
by John Smylie

Bones

Growing up in the suburbs, I didn't have a lot of opportunity to come across bones. Yes of course there were bones for dogs, steak bones, and milk bones, but I didn't run into a lot of bones in the manicured yards of friends and neighbors. Occasionally I would run into a dead mouse brought home to be admired by one of our Siamese cats but then one really only saw a limp and fleshy body of those poor creatures.

In the summers, we would head for the wilderness. As a family, we would pack up the station wagon with the rear seat facing out the back window. Dad would have one of the boats that he made during the winter trailing behind and we would drive for over eight hours through the Appalachian Mountains on the way to New Hampshire. We were very blessed to be able to rent a cottage on a beautiful and primitive lake. The cottage, also called a camp, was very rustic. The main room surrounded the large fireplace and at one end there was a staircase that led up to the second floor on which there was a balcony that surrounded the entire living room. There were several bedrooms and bathrooms off the balcony. At the far ends of the second floor and visible from the living room there were two large heads. One was of a moose the other appeared to be a very large buck. On the second floor across from the fireplace there was a skull. I never was quite sure what it was and I think that was my first experience of old dry bones. It's probably a good thing that the Lord didn't come into that space and stir up those old bones, certainly I would have been terrified as a child to see that moose or that deer or that skull come off the wall and come alive.

Several years ago, my wife had an encounter with bones. It was an autumn day and I was in my home office working on a church project when from the garage I heard her scream, calling me to come. I don't remember ever having heard her sound so shaken up before. I had no idea what it was that she could be screaming about. I left my office immediately and found her trembling in the garage pointing to a little skull on the floor next to our five-month-old puppy. He had brought home what he thought was a treasure from the woods.

Earlier that year Jill's faithful golden retriever of many years had to be put down. He was suffering greatly and could no longer even get up on his legs. We have a veterinarian who lives across the street from us in our home in Spokane who came over and took a look at Buddy. After a few moments, he recommended to us that we take him and have him put to sleep. He couldn't do it for us at our own home; we had to go to a local veterinarian who performed the task. The veterinarian asked if we would like to be with him when he died I said yes as did our youngest child; Jill declined. We went in and had Buddy put to sleep. He had been such a fine animal — polite, respectful, and he would never enter the house without first being invited. It felt right to assist him in his last journey and though it was difficult, we both were glad to be in the room with him when he breathed his last breath.

In the springtime of that year, I decided that I would surprise Jill with a new puppy. I looked through the paper over the course of a couple weeks until it appeared that there would be a good selection of puppies for us to look at. Though there's no way of replacing one living creature with another, we knew that we liked golden retrievers and there was a new litter of golden retrievers with eight puppies available to pick out and pick up. We drove from Spokane into northern

Idaho and found a humble home with a tired-looking mother golden retriever caring for eight lively little creatures. After spending time with each one of the puppies, we decided on a particular male that seemed to have a subdued personality. There was something quite aristocratic about his nature and we thought he would be a bit easier to raise than some of the other more rambunctious little personalities that were running around on four legs.

We brought him home and named him Reilly. I don't know why we named him that it just felt right at the time. He was an excellent puppy. I will always remember the first time I put him on a leash and we walked down to the mailbox, which is a mile away from our home. Never once did he tug on the leash, the entire time he was on my right keeping in perfect step. I couldn't believe how well mannered and how adult he was behaving. Reilly enjoyed sleeping in the garage. One evening he disappeared. We wondered if perhaps someone had taken him. We also knew that there were coyotes in the area and we wondered if the coyotes had gotten hold of him during the night. I kept hoping he would return, but hours turned into days, and days turned into weeks, and we knew that Reilly would not be returning.

At the end of summer, I took one of our children and went off on an evening adventure and found another little golden retriever puppy that I brought home. We named him RJ, which stands for Reilly Jr. He was a lot different than the original Reilly; in fact he still is. He is anything but aristocratic. The first time he went on a leash he pulled me the entire time. He's a sweetheart of an animal but far less disciplined than his namesake though over time he has grown to be better behaved. Our house in Spokane has a good deal of wooded area all around it. As RJ grew older, he enjoyed exploring the woods. On this particular day, the day that I heard Jill screaming in the garage, RJ had brought home a skull. Looking at the skull, I knew immediately that he had solved the mystery of Reilly's death. It was Reilly's skull that RJ brought back to our garage. That sweet life was now represented by a dry bone.

As sad as it was to discover that Reilly had died such a cruel death most likely by coyotes, it was also good to know what had happened to him. We now knew better how to pray for him, even at the time of his death, praying that his suffering was minimal, hoping that he would know our care for him even as he faced the horrors that sometimes occur in the natural world. I'm not sure bones are ever pleasant to come across because they represent a life that is no longer with us. I am sure that our Lord breathes life into our bones. Some of us may feel we have old bones that could use a little of the Spirit's breath upon us. Ezekiel lets us know that even the old dry bones, lost bones, and forgotten bones, the bones covered by sand and bleached by the sun, these old bones can have new life breathed into them.

Perhaps today as we reflect upon the good news that we find in the Spirit breathing life into the old bones that lay in the tomb, or bones that are scattered in the woods or bleached white under the desert sun, perhaps we can find hope in the deaths we have faced in our lifetime, knowing and believing that our Lord is able to reconstruct, bring alive, renew, refresh, and even cause old bones to be reborn. I think in God's time I'll get to see Buddy again, and Reilly who lived for such a short time, and my dad who lived a faithful life, and my grandfather who used to play with me when I was a little boy and my first wife who was a soul mate. All these who have gone before, who now are little more than bone and ash, I believe can and will have the Spirit blow upon them and on the last day they will arise and join in the triumphal procession through the pearly gates and walk upon the golden streets of heaven.

Passion / Palm Sunday
Matthew 26:14—27:66
by David O. Bales

Is It Truth?

Near the city of Rome in the year later numbered 49 AD, Aaron's father brought Aaron, then ten years old, to a synagogue where they'd never been. Only male believers in Jesus were summoned. They received two days' notice: "Every male member of a household believing in Christ must arrive at the synagogue in the port city of Ostia by midday."

As soon as Aaron and his father entered the synagogue, his father pointed Aaron to the other boys and told him to wait with them. His father joined the thirty or so men speaking softly as they huddled in a corner. Aaron was pleased to see Caleb among the other boys. Caleb was two years older than Aaron and he made it his business to answer all of Aaron's questions. "What's going on?" Aaron asked. "Abba just said we had to come but he didn't say why."

"Something about the emperor," Caleb said. He looked around quickly. "When we left home early this morning Imma was crying."

"My Imma hugged me so hard it hurt," Aaron said.

Caleb began to say, "Abba thinks they might want us out of the city so they can..." when the synagogue's front door opened. Four fully equipped soldiers entered, leading an old man. For a few heartbeats no Jew moved or spoke. One soldier stepped forward and announced in Latin and then repeated himself in Greek, "Over here. Listen to this man." The Jewish males turned toward the soldiers and the old man with them. The old man was dressed as a Jew. Aaron scurried to his father's side, glancing at the soldiers' swords as he did.

The soldiers stepped back and blocked the door. A few men turned to look at the other door. Soldiers had stepped in quietly from the back also. The adults all looked around desperately. The old man raised his hand and spoke, "Peace. Peace," he said in Aramaic. "It is well. It is well."

Aaron could tell that his father's hearing the man speak in Aramaic helped him relax a little.

"I've been sent by Emperor Claudius, savior of the world, benefactor of humankind, patron of art and reverence. May he prosper and may sacrifices in Jerusalem continue to be offered for his well-being."

The Jewish men shuffled their feet or looked down at this description of the emperor, but all remained silent.

"I've come to remind us Jews how reverently and benevolently the empire has treated us. We are exempted from military service, are we not? Our obedience to the holy sabbath is honored, is it not? And even though many of us dwell in Rome because Pompey brought our great-grandfathers here as slaves, we witness to how quickly our people here have been granted freedom."

The old man paused and stroked his beard. "Now, however, some of you have provoked other Jews to riot because of this Jesus. So the government that protects all lands and seas informs you now for your own good about the Jesus you call Messiah. The truth that our faithful auxiliary legions reported nearly a generation ago is that a man named Jesus Barabbas was crucified in Jerusalem by Pilate — not Jesus of Nazareth. Barabbas was a great hero of our people. He offered himself in place of the Nazarene, who was a simple country teacher who in Jerusalem found himself confused when opposition mounted and his supporters abandoned him."

Aaron looked up at his father who held his lips tightly shut and his eyes straight forward.

"An unfortunate misunderstanding arose that Jesus of Nazareth was killed and was magically restored to the living.

This mistaken report has been twisted twenty different ways by 100 fools around the sea in the middle of the inhabited world. The certified report states that Jesus died a few years later in Bethlehem and some of his sincere and grief-stricken students snatched his body from his family and buried him not in a tomb, but in a grave in the Essene cemetery by the Dead Sea. His grave remains there beside that of his Uncle Zechariah for anyone to inspect."

Aaron's thoughts were pounding through his ten-year-old head. He had learned that Jesus suffered and that God resurrected him, proving he was the Messiah. Aaron nudged his father's hand to ask a question, but his father shushed him.

The old man began to speak slower, pausing between each word, "Remember, I tell you this as the Emperor's messenger... with your safety in the balance."

Without another word or gesture, he turned and the soldiers with him followed as he exited. The soldiers who had been at the rear door, instead of leaving as they came, paraded through the synagogue to leave by the front door.

To Aaron the gasps and sighs that followed sounded as though everyone started to breathe again. He grabbed his Father's hand firmly this time and tugged him down. "Abba, is it truth?"

A man was speaking to his father on his other side and everyone was moving quickly toward the synagogue's door. His father pulled Aaron hastily from the building as he said, "Son, if Jesus hasn't been raised from the dead, you can say that anything is true. Now hang on to Abba's hand."

Aaron held tightly as other grandfathers, fathers, and sons scurried toward home. He and Caleb saw one another as their fathers yanked them into different groups scurrying back toward Rome. Before they lost sight of each other, Aaron and Caleb gave one another a confused wave.

Maundy Thursday
1 Corinthians 11:23-26
by C. David McKirachan

Do This Remembering Me...

Sometimes I wonder how we've gotten to the stilted ceremonial enactment of the fellowship meal that was the beginning and the core of the Christian experience. We use starched linens and little shot glasses loaded into silver trays like bullets into a magazine. Then there's the cubed wonder bread. I worry sometimes that in our effort to be faithful to the Lord, we forget him by making this gift of sharing he gave us into a dry ritual.

What are we supposed to remember? We're supposed to remember him. We're supposed to remember his life — his vibrant, real, messy life. We're supposed to remember his passion to share the glory of God's presence in every moment, in spite of the obtuseness of his friends and followers. We're supposed to remember his insistence on pushing his disciples closer to each other and closer to God, in spite of their desires to be individuals and run their own agendas and maintain control. We're supposed to remember his compassion and empathy that realized and understood all the hang-ups and fears and foibles of these people who sat around him, and his forgiveness and deep, deep hope for their growth beyond all the idiocies. We're supposed to remember his joy at the smallest and most glorious bits and pieces of life. We're supposed to remember his sorrow and grief at the shadows that they preferred to the light of all that glory. And we're supposed to remember his love that infused each and every word he said and movement he made.

Does all of that come through our ritual? Does he stand in our midst?

No. And yes.

The mystery of our feast is not in our excellence but in his presence. We're no better than they were. We're obtuse and confused and hung up and angry and judgmental and controlling and afraid and self-centered and hard-hearted, just like they were — and he still comes among us. Once in a while, as the bread is broken, his hand scarred by our sin, rests on our shoulder and calls us beloved.

And we remember him.

Good Friday
Isaiah 52:13—53:12
by Frank Ramirez

Reflecting Martyrs

> *Surely he has borne our infirmities and carried our diseases; yet we accounted him stricken, struck down by God, and afflicted. He was wounded for our transgressions, crushed for our iniquities; upon him was the punishment that made us whole, and by his bruises we are healed.*
> — Isaiah 53:4-5

In the eyes of some people, the Amish are the stuff of postcards, quaint men with long beards and women in black bonnets riding horse and buggy as a vague rejection of modernism. It is often forgotten by tourists that their lifestyle is based on their fierce commitment to live every aspect of their lives as disciples of Jesus. "What would Jesus do?" is not a slogan for a bracelet but a question that is not only asked but also answered and then lived.

If any were ignorant of this fact they were simply not paying attention after the killing of five Amish girls at the Nickel Mines schoolhouse on October 2, 2006, referred to by the Amish as their own 9/11.

One of the most striking aspects of the Nickel Mines murders was the way the families of the victims and the Amish at large immediately visited the family of the murderer and extended forgiveness and grace. They also shared a portion of the financial contributions that came streaming in from around the world with the killer's family.

Also memorable was the way one of the older girls in the one-room schoolhouse told the murderer to shoot her first. Her intent was to allow others to live by dying first.

To the Amish this self-sacrifice, this willingness to die for others, comes as naturally as the ability to forgive. For them this is what it means to take the Sermon on the Mount seriously. If scripture were not enough, Amish children grow up with stories from the immense volume known as *The Martyr's Mirror*, stories that make such actions automatic.

The Martyr's Mirror, published in 1660, tells the story of those Christians, including Mennonites and other Anabaptists, who died at the hands of other Christians because they chose to serve Jesus rather than acknowledge the lordship of Caesar. The book connects the suffering of faithful Christians who chose to be baptized as adults rather than be part of the state churches of Europe, with the faithfulness of martyrs in all ages. You will find a copy of this book in nearly all Amish homes.

One of the most famous stories, well known to Amish children and told as an example of the selfless love that all Christians should have, is that of Dirk Willems. In the year 1569, Dirk was arrested by the religious authorities in Asperen, Holland, for having held Bible studies in his home and for having been baptized as an adult. The account of his arrest follows:

> *Concerning his apprehension, it is stated by trustworthy persons, that when he fled he was hotly pursued by a thiefcatcher, and as there had been some frost, said Dirk Willems ran before over the ice, getting across with considerable peril. The thiefcatcher following him broke through, when Dirk Willems, perceiving that the former was in danger of his life, quickly returned and aided him in getting out, and thus saved his life. The thiefcatcher wanted to let him go, but the burgomaster, very sternly called to him to consider his oath, and thus he was again seized by the thiefcatcher, and, at said place, after severe imprisonment and great trials ... put to death at a lingering fire by these bloodthirsty, ravening wolves, enduring it with great steadfastness,*

> *and confirming the genuine faith of the truth with his death and blood, as an instructive example to all pious Christians of this time.*

Having saved his rescuer, Dirk Willems endured a particularly gruesome death. *The Martyr's Mirror* notes:

> *In this connection, it is related as true from the trustworthy memoirs of those who were present at the death of this pious witness of Jesus Christ, that the place where this offering occurred was without Asperen, on the side of Leerdam, and that, a strong east wind blowing that day, the kindled fire was much driven away from the upper part of his body, as he stood at the stake; in consequence of which this good man suffered a lingering death, insomuch that in the town of Leerdam, toward which the wind was blowing, he was heard to exclaim over seventy times: "O my Lord; my God," etc., for which cause the judge or bailiff, who was present on horseback, filled with sorrow and regret at the man's sufferings, wheeled about his horse, turning his back toward the place of execution, and said to the executioner: "Dispatch the man with a quick death." But how or in what manner the executioner then dealt with this pious witness of Jesus, I have not been able to learn, except only, that his life was consumed by the fire, and that he passed through the conflict with great steadfastness, having commended his soul into the hands of God.*

For Amish children, Dirk Willems and other men and women like him are as real as George Washington and Abraham Lincoln are to what they refer to as "the English," their term for non-Amish. The stories of *The Martyr's Mirror* bring to life those who have practiced nonresistance to evil and self-sacrifice even to the point of death for others. The example of Jesus is not just theoretical — Amish children know that his example on Calvary's hill has been emulated by thousands and thousands.

As we begin to contemplate the sacrifice of Jesus let us also think about what stories in our lives, if any, ever really challenge us to truly follow in his footsteps.

Source: Donald B. Kraybill, Steven M. Nolt, and David L. Weaver-Zercher, *Amish Grace: How Forgiveness Transcended Tragedy* (San Francisco: John Wiley & Sons, 2007)

You can download *The Martyr's Mirror* at www.martyrsmirror.com.

Easter Sunday
Acts 10:34-43; Colossians 3:1-4
by Argile Smith

Anticipation

Coach Clark had led the men's basketball team to one of the biggest winning streaks in the high school's recent memory, even though the beginning of the season had been tough. That's when two of the starters had to be sidelined. Without them, the season looked bleak. The new players who had moved into their places seemed to have some problems adjusting to the others on the team. They couldn't make themselves fit well into the team's routine or rhythm. Over and over, Coach Clark tried to fix the problem caused by the new players, but nothing worked. Consequently, he feared that the team would be doomed to one tragic loss after another and that the remainder of the season would be characterized by gut-wrenching misery for everyone involved.

Not long into the season, however, things began to click for the team. Much to Coach Clark's surprise, the team started to work together and hit a rhythm that produced points on the scoreboard. By the end of the season, the team had gained momentum with a winning spree and had almost made it all the way to the championship game. Although they didn't get as far as the championship, the guys on the team felt good about what would happen next season.

The anticipation continued to grow after the season ended. Conversations among students, teachers, parents, and other people in the community revolved around what would happen next year. The more they talked about it, the more they speculated about how many games they would win.

Their speculations fueled their excitement over the possibility of a winning season and a shot at the championship.

When Coach Clark gathered the team for training just before the new season commenced, he knew that everyone was still talking about what lay ahead. The hope of a winning season filled the air, and he knew it.

After he gave the players a chance to warm up on the court, he blew his whistle and called for everyone to take a seat on the bleachers near him. They reacted like winning players, eagerly finding their seats and situating themselves to listen to what their coach had to say to them.

Coach Clark started by thanking each of the players for staying with the team another year. He went on to affirm their talents, their fine finish last season, and the sense of anticipation regarding the future of the team. Then he elaborated on the tough beginning they endured and the happy ending they enjoyed together.

"Men," he explained, "the team came back to life after everyone had given us up for dead. When we started to come alive, people began to believe in us again. Now they're sure that we have a winning season on our hands."

After a long pause, he asserted, "But men, we're not back in last season when things started to turn around for us. And we're not playing the championship game yet either. Right now we're in the middle, somewhere between having the breath put back in our lungs last season and winning the championship next season. If what happened in the past means anything to us and if we anticipate something good happening in the future, we've got to make the most of the time in the middle."

That's when he instructed them to practice the plays more, work the court better, and shoot the ball with more accuracy. After talking about what he wanted to accomplish during pre-season training, he said, "Remember that we've experienced a resurrection of sorts. We believe that the season ahead of us looks promising. Now keep on telling yourself that you have an opportunity right now to make the most of what's here in the middle."

The resurrection of Christ breathed new life into his followers, and we anticipate a promising future because of it. The anticipation of Easter helps us as we live productively for him right now, somewhere in the middle.

Easter 2
John 20:19-31
by Keith Hewitt

Tracks

It had snowed again — a late season dusting, a thin layer of fresh powder like a clean, white sheet thrown over the bones of Old Man Winter. They stepped out onto the stoop, and as the man pulled the door shut his son leaned over and studied two lines of markings in the snow. "What's that?" he asked, pointing at the tracks in the pristine white snow.

His father glanced at his watch, then looked down at the tracks. Each line was like a series of dots, almost one in front of the other. Looking closer, the dots resolved into four-toed paw prints; looking closer still, the procession of prints actually formed a kind of double line, with the paw prints marching silently on either side of an imaginary line. "Those are cat tracks," he said, and pointed with a gloved finger. "See how each one is almost in front of the one behind it, alternating to one side or the other? That's how cats walk."

"Must be a big cat," his son judged. "The paws are almost a foot apart." He pointed back, to where the tracks came around the corner of the house and then cut through the yard, across the stoop, down the sidewalk, and onto the driveway — perfectly parallel and rail-straight.

"I don't think so," the father answered, "Come on." They walked to the driveway, the boy taking care not to step on the tracks. They got to the driveway, and he said, "See, there."

The left line of prints peeled off suddenly, going down the driveway between the clear spot where his wife's van and his daughter's car had been parked. The other line went around the front of his daughter's car, then cut down between her car and his. "It's two cats!" the boy said excitedly, and ran the couple of steps to where the tracks split. "See! This one went down there, and this one went over by your car!" As he talked, the words came out in puffs of clouds, warm breath expelled into cold air.

"Looks that way," his father agreed.

"Were they chasing one another?"

"I don't think so — the stride doesn't seem to be very long." He glanced at his watch again, then in spite of himself looked around the driveway. "Here," he said, after a moment. He walked down the driveway to where the van had been parked, stepping in the clear space, stopping at the end nearest the street. His son hurried over to where he stood, looked down at the tracks in the snow, where he pointed.

"A rabbit?" the boy wondered, gauging the short stretch of tracks coming from under a bush — this was a pattern of two long prints, side by side, with a pair of smaller prints between them and toward the back, almost one in front of the other. If he closed his eyes, he could almost see it hop out from under the bush, cross the bit of driveway to the van, and then disappear under it.

But where to, then? He looked around, walked to the other end of the clear spot, now slowly starting to get covered with an airbrushing of white, fluffy snow as the wind picked up. There! "He went under the van here, then came out from under by the tire at the other end — back toward the garage."

"Yep," his father agreed. "Maybe trying to dodge the cats." He nodded toward the car, then. "Let's go, or we'll be late."

Reluctantly, his son walked back to the car, eyes scanning as his head swiveled from side to side, trying to spot the animals. As he crossed in front of his father's car, he stopped, stared at the hood for a moment, then laughed and pointed. "Looks like someone else was here too!"

His father paused from opening the door, looked at the hood. A line of paw prints started in the middle, appearing out of nowhere, then proceeded down to the front left corner, back across the hood, up to the windshield, and off. These were a series of "V" shapes, two four-toed prints in the back, two larger five-toes prints in the front.

"Was it another cat?" his son wondered.

"I don't think so. They're too small, and not the right shape." He looked around, then looked up — and nodded. "Those are squirrel tracks. See, it came out on that branch, there —" he pointed to a thick, leafless branch hanging over his car, "— jumped down on the car, then ran around and jumped off."

"Cool! Maybe he was avoiding the cats too."

"Maybe. Now let's get going, or we'll be late for church."

All the way there, the boy talked about the tracks they had found, even as the wind peeled the evidence off the car's hood and dusted over that which was left behind at home. His mother was just finishing her meeting as they arrived, and he ran up to hug her. "Mom!" he said excitedly, "we had all kinds of animals running around our house this morning!"

"Really? I didn't see any animals when I left for church."

"Neither did we," he said, "but we know they were there — we saw the tracks!"

"Then it's just like God," she said.

"What do you mean?" he asked.

"I mean you never really see him — but you can look at what he's done in the world around you, and know he's been there."

The reality of our faith is that only a handful of followers ever saw the risen Savior. We can cluck our tongues at

Thomas, and chide him for doubting because he hadn't seen — but in the end, we are not that different. We have not seen the wounds, put our hands in the holes, but we do not believe without proof, either.

It's just a different kind of proof — a faith-driven proof.

We see the proof of God's love in the world around us. Every act of mercy, every kindness of one human to another, every moment of grace comes about because God touches the human heart, and the heart acts. We feel the power of God's love inside us, the energy and peace that should not go together, but somehow do, as they fill the void in our souls left by sin.

We do not need to touch Jesus' wounds, because we can touch our own, and wonder at the healing that God has wrought in us... and know that Jesus is among us still.

Easter 3
Acts 2:14a, 22-32
by John Smylie

Speak the Truth in Love

Peter, standing with the eleven, raised his voice and addressed them: "Therefore let the entire house of Israel know with certainty that God has made him both Lord and Messiah, this Jesus whom you crucified."

It seems to me there is a temptation among Christians to be nice. Peter, in addressing this crowd is anything but nice. He loves, but he is not nice.

It takes a lot of confidence to be able to speak the truth without the fear of repercussions. Peter has come to that place having experienced the depth of his own weakness. It wasn't that long ago that he denied his Lord three times when his Lord was in his most vulnerable moments. Peter has obviously done a whole lot of growing since then and now he himself was willing to put himself at risk to speak the truth.

I have a friend who has a gift of being able to speak the truth in love, in pastoral situations, from the pulpit and in almost every walk of life. Somehow those, at least most of those who hear him, love the fact that he is willing to challenge them. I think they love him because they know that he cares for them and is willing to risk his own relationship with them because he loves them so much. He is the best pastor I have ever met. I have known him to confront the powerful and the meek. I have known him to confront bishops, fellow clergy, government officials, and others.

There was one time when he was at a funeral of a friend who was being buried from a Roman Catholic church. My friend is an Episcopal clergyman and he was dressed in his clerical collar while attending a service. He had no role in conducting the service. He simply was one of those who sits in the pew to worship the Lord, pray for the family, and care for those in attendance while honoring the departed. When it was time to receive communion only the Roman Catholics in attendance at the service were invited to receive the sacrament. Apparently, these are the rules. Something inside my friend got stirred up and he felt called to come forward and receive the sacrament. For him the sacrament meant being connected not only with Christ but with the gathered community and with the departed. For him to skip the sacramental meal that was being offered would have been an insult to the family of his friend and to his friend whose life they had gathered to celebrate. So he disregarded the instruction of the priest — that this was for Roman Catholics only — and he came forward and knelt at the altar rail with hands stretched out to receive the Body of Christ.

When the Roman Catholic priest came by he refused to give the sacrament to my friend. My friend then said to him, "You have to give it to me." The priest again refused. My friend then said to him, "If this is the Body of Christ, you have to give it to me." My friend wasn't going anywhere. The Catholic priest was becoming angry. My friend then asked him, "Is this just some Roman Catholic thing or is it the Body of Christ? If it's the Body of Christ you must give it to me." The Catholic priest then placed the sacrament in my friend's hand saying to him, "You will see me in my office after the service." I don't know what happened in the office but I do know that my friend spoke the truth with love to the Roman priest and perhaps even to the Catholic church. It didn't matter to him if it was a local priest, the bishop, or even the Pope administering the sacrament. What mattered to him was the connection that was found in the bread and in the wine — a connection to the living God — a connection to the community gathered — a connection to the God of the living — a connection to his departed friend.

Some of us come by this talent naturally — the talent of speaking the truth in love — others of us, like Peter, may learn this the hard way. Early on in my ministry, I was more concerned with being liked than I was with speaking the truth. I hadn't named that within myself at that time but later I came to learn that this was true — one of my weaknesses — one of my flaws. When we discover we are among those who were more interested in being liked and pleasing others than we are in speaking the truth in love, we may discover that we have an opportunity to grow. Being nice and seeking to please others rather than speaking the truth in love leads to a very empty and hollow feeling and certainly does nothing to advance Christianity.

As we learn this lesson — as we risk speaking the truth in love — we become more substantive — more whole — more like Christ. I recently had an opportunity to speak the truth in love to an older gentleman who was making life-and-death decisions.

Roger was in and out of the hospital. Over the last several months it seemed that he was spending more and longer stays there. The quality of his life was deteriorating and he was afraid that he was becoming a burden to all those around him, especially his wife, Doris. His heart was failing. The medications that he was taking were becoming more difficult to manage. The internal defibrillator had become a burden that he no longer wanted to bear. His life was slowly ebbing away and he was growing more frustrated with the experience.

After much reflection, discussion with family, his doctors, and his priest, Roger decided that he was ready to stop treatment. To continue on would be to continue on the same path — the same downward spiral — more time in the hospital, less time at home — and he was unwilling to stay on that path. He made the decision to turn off the internal defibrillator and to wean himself away from the medications. He now would qualify for hospice care. He lived in a community that had a residential hospice unit — a home that he could move into and spend his last days under hospice care. His family could visit as often as they liked — unlimited visiting hours. In his mind, he wanted to make the transition from this life to the next as easy for his wife Doris as he could. He did not want to burden her even though hospice would offer on-site care for him if he chose to go to his home.

Doris was very clear that she wanted Roger to come home and die in the place that he loved, surrounded by family and the normalcy of everyday life. She wanted to be near him and have him hear the sounds of grandchildren in the house, breathe the aroma of wonderful meals being prepared in the kitchen, and experience the normalcy of the ordinary where God may be found most often. Roger didn't want to hear anything of this; he was determined to make life easier for Doris, and he was convinced he knew better. This is where I was invited to enter the conversation. This is where I felt I was called to speak the truth in love to my friend Roger. I had already affirmed his decision to put himself in God's care and allow himself to retreat from the extraordinary medical care that he was receiving. We had spent time reflecting on death as a part of life. What I needed to do here was to challenge Roger to receive the kindness, compassion, dedication, and love of his wife. He was being stubborn and, of course, the temptation was to pity him because of his situation. I did not pity him; in fact I believe with God's grace I was able to speak to him truth in love. When I challenged Roger to stop being so stubborn and listen to his wife and receive her deep and abiding love for him and go home and die there, he looked at me and smiled.

Roger received the word of his priest. Roger received the grace and kindness and compassion and love of his wife.

Roger has been received into the gracious and loving arms of his Lord.

Peter spoke the truth with love to those who had rejected Jesus. He told them of their mistake, perhaps knowing full well that he himself might be a victim of the same cruelty his Lord experienced — the same rejection — even a similar death. Peter was willing to give these folks a chance to do the right thing — a chance to turn around, a chance to repent, a chance to experience the good news of the risen Lord for themselves.

Speaking the truth in love really is all about caring for another. Our Lord's entire life is a witness to speaking the truth in love, and each of us is invited to join in his great mission with all that we say, with all that we do, with all that we have, and with all that we are.

Easter 4
Psalm 23
by C. David McKirachan

Familiar Words

The 23rd Psalm is good stuff. It says deep and meaningful things about God and about us. It confronts, comforts, and assures. Yup. But there is something more about this one. It sings in a voice that resonates deeper than any meaningful words could reach. There is something about the cadence and the touch of "The Lord is my shepherd..." that reminds us of who we are in a way that other, just as profound words do not.

She was in the nursing home when I moved here, more than a decade ago. She had been "out of it" for years before that. She didn't know anyone and sat and stared into some distance beyond the horizons I could see. Then she lost what consciousness she had and slipped into a coma. I went to see her once in a while. I'd sit and talk to her. Tell her things that were going on with her friends and in the church.

One evening I got a call that she wasn't "long for this world." As I drove over, I wondered where she'd been all these years, between here and there. I wondered if she had to come back to leave. I wondered...

The nurse told me she'd been peaceful, but her breathing had changed and her vitals were dropping. I leaned over and smoothed back her hair, as I'd done before and came close to her ear. I whispered, "Wherever you've been, or wherever you're going, you're going with God." And I started whispering "The Lord is my shepherd..." She straightened in bed and opened her eyes, not wide, but wide enough to see me. And she started softly saying the psalm with me. She was hoarse, it had been a long time since she used that voice, but she stuck to it.

When we got to "...forever," she closed her mouth and smiled, a soft and satisfied smile and then closed her eyes and settled in. I heard the nurse move and looked up. She almost stuttered, "She hasn't spoken in years." "Well, maybe she finally had something important to say."

I don't know what circuit the psalm closed. I don't care if it reminded her of her childhood or her hope. I do know that something in those words and that rhythm called to her through all the fog and cobwebs and let her connect. She died an hour later, slipping off into an untroubled sleep.

It's good stuff, that psalm. Better than we know.

Easter 5
John 14:1-14
by Scott Dalgarno

Please Don't Forget Me

When we visit my wife's father, Henry (Hank, as everybody knows him), it's my job to prepare the scrambled eggs. On the particular morning I'm remembering, the day after Thanksgiving, I crack the eggs while my daughter Sarah cuts fruit into bowls — no grapefruit for her mother, lots of melon for her brother, and extra banana for her grandfather. I try hard to make sure the eggs are not runny, but not dry either.

Soon everyone is seated at the family table made by Hank himself. There's a chair for everyone and one chair set aside for Hank's late wife, Edith, my children's most beloved grandmother. The cushion is covered with fabric from one of her cheery summer dresses.

"Who's the boy?" Hank asks, looking directly at our son. "That's your grandson, Stephen," my wife, Catherine says. Hank doesn't recognize any of us anymore, except, Catherine. Hank has had a series of strokes — the last one took most of his memory and has left his right side shriveled. The one thing his memory is clear on is Edith. She was the one thing in his life that really "worked." "Best decision I ever made," he used to say, and now he can't even remember what he did all his life, what a difference he made in the lives of so many young people at Syracuse University.

The family tradition was that Hank says grace at meals, which I used to find funny because until he was nearly sixty, he was a self-described agnostic. It was the realization, coming on the eve of old age, that he and Edith would not always be together (on this side of the grave) that made him begin to entertain the idea of heaven.

Maybe it was because she was such a beacon of goodness that he began to think the existence of such a place was even possible. Oh, there was nothing all that saintly about her. No, she had a wicked sense of humor — everyone knew that. But she was just so... so solid. Her integrity was absolute. She was the one person I've met in my life who really loved everybody. Some try, but Edith pulled it off, and there was no doubting it. I remember how suspect I was, meeting this amazing family the day that Catherine first brought me into her home. To Hank, I was Charles Manson until proven otherwise. But not for Edith. She read in the looks Catherine gave me at our first dinner around this same table that I was someone special, even if I didn't feel it myself, and until the day of her death she made me feel that I had given her the greatest two gifts in her life — her two grandchildren.

It was the day she died when something broke, for the first time, in Hank's steely composure. We all stood or sat around Grandma's bed and we were holding her hands, chatting quietly, and she just slipped away, as they say. No great labored breaths, no rattles, just a quiet letting go. We found ourselves transfixed by the smile that came to her mouth and eyes in that last moment. It wasn't lost on Hank. Whatever she was seeing, HE wanted to see. More than that, he wanted to go where she had told him she believed she was headed — the place she was sure she would see her own mother again, and the place she believed she would see the one who taught her it was possible to love people as if they were all children of God.

For Hank, heaven became a matter of trust, of trusting his wife. In those few moments beside her bed, his heart grew strangely warm. Where she was going, he wanted to go, and his sarcasm about spiritual matters evaporated right then and there.

Once the eggs and bowls of fruit were placed in front of everyone we bowed our heads, grabbed hands, and waited. Hank didn't speak. After a few moments of silence Catherine began, "God is..." Hank chimed in, "God is..." That was followed by another long pause, at which point Stephen and Sarah started in slowly and deliberately. "God is good, God is great. Let us thank him for our food." Everyone added an "Amen" except Hank. He still had his head bowed. He seemed to be mumbling something. Catherine leaned over kissing his shoulder and rubbing his back very gently. Then she raised herself and settled her head on his shoulder looking about eighteen again. It nearly did me in.

After breakfast Catherine and I gathered up the dishes. I noticed tears in her eyes. "Are you all right?" I asked.

She hesitated and then said, "Dad was praying the same thing over and over. He just kept saying, 'God take care of Edith,' and 'God... please don't forget me. Please don't forget me. Please don't forget me....'"

Easter 6
Acts 17:22-31
by Peter Andrew Smith

Looking for God

There once was a man who wanted more in life. He believed there must be something greater than what he was experiencing, some grander purpose than just surviving day to day, some deeper meaning to connect to in his life, so he began to search.

He spent time considering the world around him and discovered that when he was outside in nature he felt connected to something greater than himself. Sitting on the seashore or watching the sunrise on a mountain, he felt something he did not feel in his everyday life. He wanted to experience and know that feeling all the time but could never control when it occurred.

The man tried to find what he sought by achieving perfect health. He exercised, ate healthy, and he stretched the limits of his body. As he engaged in physical activity, he discovered there were times when he felt alive like no other. Yet those occasions were fleeting and those times never lasted long.

The man who was searching tried to understand. He studied, researched, and learned. As he expanded his mind, he experienced occasions when he caught a glimpse of something more. At those times, he felt that he was close to what he was seeking, but those occasions also never lasted. No matter how much he studied and learned he could not truly understand what he sought.

The man used what he had seen in nature, what he had learned, and what he could do, to create. He fashioned things in words, paint, and clay. As the man created, he sometimes felt connected to what he sought. In the sentences, in the pictures from his imagination, as his hands sculpted, he felt more than himself but he was never able to completely capture what he desired in his art.

The man assumed he had failed in his search. He looked at what he had seen, felt, understood, and achieved and knew now more than ever that there was something missing in his life.

One day the man came upon another man and shared his story. He told of his searching, his desire to know the greater life, which always seemed just beyond him. The other man listened to the story of searching and told him of the God who had created all the earth, who fashioned humanity in the divine image, who knew everything and who was the source of inspiration and imagination. The man who had searched was excited as he heard of this God for he knew that the glimpses of something greater he had known in life must be of God.

When the other man told him that God had come to earth so that everyone could see, understand, and know God, the man began to weep. As he wept, he began to see the hand of God in the world around him, in the life he felt within him, in the understanding he had of the universe, and in the creativity he expressed. He dried his tears and realized he no longer had to search for God because God had found him.

Ascension of Our Lord
Acts 1:1-11
by Argile Smith

Wayne's Deployment

Wayne had his orders in his duffle bag when he walked through the door into Todd's room. A soldier who wanted to make a career out of military service, he knew that soon enough he would get an overseas assignment. That's why his deployment to Afghanistan didn't surprise him.

Being single made the assignment a little easier because he wouldn't leave behind a wife or children. Leaving his mom and dad and especially Todd, his little brother, turned out to be difficult enough. Going upstairs and walking through the door to Todd's bedroom to tell him good-bye tore at his heart.

He and Todd sat on the floor and talked about the assignment. Wayne reassured his little brother that he would return safe and sound. They talked about what they would do while they were separated and what they would do together once he came home. And then Wayne gave Todd that kind of hug known only to brothers who care about each other.

When the time had come for Wayne to leave, he said good-bye to his mom and dad who had been waiting downstairs. Todd walked with him down the steps. When Wayne hugged his parents, picked up his duffle bag, and walked outside to his car, Todd followed him. As Wayne drove away, Todd rushed to the street and watched as the taillights faded in the distance. For a long time he just stood there. Perhaps he hoped that Wayne would turn around and come home. Or maybe he regretted that he couldn't go with Wayne.

Soon his mom joined him in the street, and the two of them stood together, weeping but saying nothing. His mom simply ran her hands through his hair like she had done so many times before when she sensed that he was upset about something. It was her way of consoling him without uttering a word. Actually, nothing could be said. Wayne had to go, and everyone who loved him had to stay.

But then she said, "Todd, Wayne's coming home. Just wait and see." And with that, the two of them walked back into the house, still weeping but now walking together in the resolve that they would be strong for each other and for Wayne.

Thanks to email messages, cell phone calls, and letters, Todd and his parents heard from Wayne more often than they anticipated. Wayne tried to keep them posted regularly on how things were going for him, the people he worked with, and — to a limited extent — the work he was doing.

A few months passed, and the family got some good news about Wayne. They found out that he had been given a promotion. Although the circumstances were sketchy, the point was clear. Wayne's superior officer recognized his potential for leadership and placed a significant number of soldiers under his command.

Not long afterward, Wayne's family found out about a commendation that he had received. Again, the information regarding the reason for the commendation was a little vague, but it had to do with meritorious service in the line of duty.

The details related to Wayne's promotion and commendation found a home in Todd's imagination. He investigated the kinds of metals and badges Wayne had been given, and he imagined them emblazoned on his brother's uniform. One day he would see Wayne coming home, bearing on his uniform all of the symbols of his success. Todd looked forward to his brother's return that much more.

The ascension of Jesus leaves with a similar batch of mixed emotions. Separation, intimacy, and expectancy blend together in our hearts to strengthen our resolve to follow him.

Easter 7
John 17:1-11
by John Smylie

Where's the Finish Line?

> *I glorified you on earth by finishing the work that you gave me to do.*
> — John 17:4

For the last several weeks, there has been an enjoyable series of articles written by two women who are part of our local newspaper. One of them is a reporter who often gets her stories on the front page — she is young, attractive, and energetic. She has served in missionary activity and always appears to be up for a challenge. The other is also young and works more behind the scenes on the editorial staff of the paper. She is married, the mother of young children, and comes across in her reports as one who is quite humble and reflective.

The two of them have decided to run a marathon. That in itself is a very noble ambition. What makes this particular pact between them even more noble is the added obstacle of running the marathon in Colorado beginning in Estes Park where the elevation is way above one mile. In other words, the air is very thin and the training must take into account the lesser oxygen that is found at a higher elevation. The two of them are writing stories about their training as they prepare for the marathon this summer. Both of them come across as rather realistic and humble, admitting the times when they fall short in their training regimen. They reflect aloud about their own humanity. They invite the reader into their journey. Both of them wonder if they will finish the race. One of them, the mom, in a recent article has begun to lower her expectations. In chatting with her children, she's come to a kind of interior compromise that suggests that if she even begins the race and runs for more than a mile it will be sort of a personal victory.

The younger of the two also shares the kind of mind games that go on inside of her head as she prepares for this overwhelming task. At times, she chooses to leave her training regimen for the allure of an afternoon nap. I think why I'm so attracted to the two storytellers is that I find myself in the midst of both of their stories. It's so easy to set lofty goals. Perhaps for many of us our marathons are goals like losing 30 pounds that have crept on us over the last several years, or setting aside time to pray at least 45 minutes to an hour a day. Some of us seek to make it a priority to spend more time with our children and less time at work, yet we continue to fall short of this seemingly simple goal. Others determine that they will become more environmentally sensitive by driving their cars less and riding their bicycles and walking more. Some of us may seek to discipline ourselves to become less compulsive in our spending habits only to fall short when we see that irresistible pair of shoes that has our name written on them. On and on the list goes, the list that many of us renew at the end of each year with New Year's resolutions that are usually forgotten by January 15.

We won't know how the two newspaper women do until the summer but every one of us is challenged with similar goals perhaps not as lofty as a marathon but nevertheless challenges that call forth the best from us. Personally I hope the two ladies make it, I hope they're able not only to compete in the marathon but to finish the race even if it takes them several hours more than they anticipate, even if they have to walk across the finish line.

Many of us wonder what we have to do to make a difference in this world of ours. I think there may be something in human nature that is constantly calling us from the comfort of our lives into something more. I believe there is something noble, excellent, engaged, and even driven in the human spirit, something that lives within each of us; perhaps it could be described as a spark of the divine that calls us, moves us, and pushes us toward the divine and toward excellence. I believe that we are each made in the image of God. Though we may not yet understand how that gets to be lived out in the midst of us or through us, I believe there is something in us, a spirit and a life that longs to be lifted up and given to the world in a way that brings glory to God.

Often throughout the years of ministry, I have encountered wonderful and humble human beings who in reflective moments have questioned their value. These are human beings who have given much of themselves to making the world a brighter and better place who nevertheless wonder if their lives really make a difference. It seems to me that these questions arise in so many, particularly in the gifted — questions of value, questions of worth — and can only be answered by the divine. When Jesus said to his Father in heaven, "I glorified you on earth by finishing the work that you gave me to do," I believe he was referring not only to the work that he had done but to the work that he knew was in front of him.

Our Lord had begun his marathon when he was baptized in the Jordan River by his friend John. He continued his marathon when he went into the wilderness and fasted for forty days and forty nights and confronted the demons and temptations that, if not confronted, could cause him to fall short of his goal. He continued his race as he gathered disciples around him so he could teach them the way of salvation through being in relationship with them. Our Lord engaged in his marathon as he traveled throughout the length of the holy land preaching the good news, giving sight to the blind, hearing to the deaf, strengthening limbs to the lame, and even giving life to the dead. Our Lord ran his race as he challenged the religious and political systems of his day by pointing to a higher way, the way of his Father in heaven, the way of peace and humility and sacrifice. Even at the time of our Lord's praying this prayer that we hear in today's gospel text, our Lord begins to see the finish line and he knows that these last few miles will be the most difficult. He knows that these last few miles, where the air is thin and the pain is excruciating, are also the most important. For our Lord it wasn't so much about winning the race as it was about finishing the race. Finishing the race for him would demand that he not only be misunderstood, but also be willing to endure great suffering, the lashes of a whip, the piercing words and spit of the arrogant, the betrayal of his friends, the agonizing death and pain of crucifixion, and the hollowness of death.

In the midst of our questions, in the midst of our wondering where is the finish line for us, let us recognize that our Lord has already completed the race. Let us be open to the truth that our Lord is reaching out to us today, praying for us not only while he was here on earth but also from the heavens. Let us open ourselves today to the strength that he alone has given us and desires for us to receive. Our Lord did not accomplish his goal by merely relying on his willpower and his human strength. Our Lord accomplished his goal by connecting to his Father in heaven — by keeping focused on the prize that was to please his Father in heaven. His desire was not for himself but to bring glory to his Father in heaven and grace to us. Let us tap into the wellspring of life who can strengthen us to finish our race. Our Lord's endurance of the marathon that was set before him was aided by the strength given him from above. The same strength is available to us. May we also be willing to receive God's call and the desire to finish the race in a way that brings satisfaction to our souls and glory to our father in heaven and grace to those around us.

Lord, you are calling us to finish the race you have put before us. Lord, you have called each of us to a unique and wonderful existence. Lord, you desire each of us to finish the race and we are well aware of our limitations. We are at times full of excuses and reasons why you have thought too highly of us. Lord, give us the grace to open ourselves to allow you to once again inspire and fill us with the divine spark, your presence, and your strength, so we may run toward the finish line you set in front of us knowing that you are lifting us, even carrying us when our legs are weak, our lungs are burning, and our minds are full of excuses. Let your heart beat within us, let your prayer carry us forward and may our lives surrender to you, giving you glory and grace to those around us.

Pentecost Sunday
1 Corinthians 12:3b-13
by John Sumwalt

A Ducky Miracle

> *Now there are a variety of gifts, but the same Spirit... To one is given through the Spirit the utterance of wisdom, and to another the utterance of knowledge according to the same Spirit, to another faith by the same Spirit, to another the gift of healing by the one Spirit, to another the working of Miracles...*
> — 1 Corinthians 12:4a, 8-10a

We had a large flock of white Muscovy ducks on the farm where I grew up in southwest Wisconsin. Duck watching was one of our favorite pastimes, especially during nesting season. Hatching time was eagerly anticipated, almost as much as Christmas and the first day of trout season.

We would check each nest daily to keep track of the number of eggs. Then came the hard part: waiting and waiting. We were not nearly as patient as the hens who did the real hard work of sitting on the nests day after day. Always just when our patience was nearly exhausted, the miracle happened. The eggs would crack one by one as the eager ducklings pecked and pushed their way out into the new world and awkwardly crawled beneath their mama's protective wings to dry and prepare themselves for the grand entrance.

There is nothing prettier than a mother duck leading her parade of yellow ducklings out into the sunlight for the first time. It is one of the miracles of God's creation. I remember that each hen seemed to beam with joy as she introduced her brood to the rest of the barnyard fowl. Some mothers had as many as 25 or 30 ducklings. Counting the fledglings in each little flock to see which mother had the most was part of the fun of duck watching.

It was also fun to watch when the mothers took them down to the creek for their first swim. The fuzzy hatchlings took to water, well, "like a duck takes to water." There was no need for special instructions, nor did the mothers have to prod them to take the plunge. Each one came gifted with the ability to glide over the surface with ease, propelled by the perpetual pumping action of their tiny webbed feet.

We had one old hen who never got to participate in these joys of motherhood. She was a different kind of duck, black and white of an unknown species, who came to us as a gift one day when the farmer up the road could no longer care for her. Penny, as we named her, would build a nest every spring and lay eggs like all of the other hens. Then she would sit on them for hours every day, for several weeks, waiting for them to hatch. But Penny's eggs never hatched. Because there were no papa ducks of her kind in our flock, Penny's eggs were infertile. Year after year, she made her nests, laid her eggs, and sat and sat on them with no result.

Eventually, Penny would give up and wait to try again the following spring. It made all of us very sad and a little angry at the injustice of it all. It didn't seem right that Penny would work so hard and be so hopeful only to be disappointed again and again. It may have been my imagination, but Penny's head seemed to droop lower and lower each year. I prayed for a miracle, as did all of the other duck watchers in our family.

Then one year it happened. To everyone's great amazement, Penny came out of the silo room, where she always had her nest, leading a dozen yellow ducklings. How happy and proud she looked. What a testament to the power of prayer.

Some months later, we learned that God had some earthly help with this ducky miracle. Mom, who was the worker of all kinds of miracles in our lives, finally confessed one day that she had carefully removed all of Penny's infertile eggs and replaced them with fertile eggs from the Muscovy hens, one from each nest. None of them seemed to notice, but all of us duck watchers couldn't help but notice the great change in Penny. She held her head high and her eyes sparkled like never before. A happier, more contented mother could not be found anywhere on the face of the earth. It didn't seem to bother Penny that none of her offspring grew up to look like her.

Holy Trinity Sunday
2 Corinthians 13:11-13
by C. David McKirachan

Benediction

When I was a kid, I received a benediction from my father every Sunday. He'd stand up there, lift his arms, and offer the blessing of benediction to his congregation, which included me. Every week it was the same one. "Now unto him who can keep you from falling and present you faultless before God and his witnesses, unto the only wise Lord our Savior be glory, majesty, dominion, and power now and forever. Amen." He mined it from various sources. It isn't necessarily perfect in form or content or poetry, but rings in my mind as the blessing that touches the deep parts of my soul. It's my father's blessing to me. It's his benediction.

When I got into the business, I decided I needed a benediction. I could have used his but I was a young and independent thinking whippersnapper who had to go his own way. So I began glomming this and that until I had something I liked and felt good about; then I repeated it at least 322 times until it wore a rut in my noggin so I could get through it even when I'm reeling from a sermon or an inspirational hymn.

So for thirty-something years I've ended services with my benediction. It makes me feel complete. It reminds me of why I'm here, doing this stuff. It also says what I want them to do with what I've been trying to preach and teach. But these last words are just a coda on the end of a service. They are a detail that I assumed no one noticed.

A friend of mine's son was getting married to a West Virginia girl. After I met her, I informed him she was too good for him. Great girl. But he's a great guy. Anyway, I was invited to the wedding in West Virginia. I drove down there a couple days early to play golf with my friend and spend time with his son. I'd baptized him and the best man when they were a lot smaller. I'd watched them tottle, run, cause enough trouble for eight kids, fought with them through confirmation, youth group, and now shook their hands, these young men who stood before me. It was a little weird not doing the wedding. But the bride was Baptist and her minister had his own agenda. So I sat in the front row with the family after I pinned their boutonnières on.

It was a beautiful wedding with candlelight and music and scripture and even a decent homily (am I a snob or what?). But at the end of it all, the groom stepped forward and asked me to come up onto the chancel. He introduced me to the congregation and then told them that through all the years he could remember I'd been his minister. He told them that he'd been a rough kid to minister to. And then he told them that through all the ups and downs of his life, whatever happiness or trouble he got into there was something he held onto and remembered no matter what. He wanted to give that back to me as a gift. And then he and the best man stepped forward and said in unison:

"Go in peace. Render unto no man or woman evil for evil. Support the weak, strengthen the fainthearted, and help the suffering, wherever you may find them. And may the grace of our Lord Jesus Christ, the love of God, and the communion and the fellowship of the Holy Spirit be and abide with each and all of you now and forever. Amen."

I stood there and cried. Big surprise. I wish I could tell my father what his benediction meant to me. I never realized until these two blew me away. Who knew? Now I have to be more careful what I say. They remember.

Proper 7 / Pentecost 2 / Ordinary Time 12
Romans 6:1b-11
by David O. Bales

Sin That Grace Abound?

Rodney said, "I just can't believe it didn't work." All his fourteen-year-old mind could dwell on was the poor execution of the plan, not the consequences that they could hear their parents' muted voices deliberating outside their bedroom. Michael, twelve years old, looked like he'd cry again soon.

Michael said, "What do you think they'll do?"

"I don't know. But think of it this way," Rodney said, "it was a great plan. It worked almost perfectly. And the parade was on time!"

Their mother had refused on a weeknight to let them go out at 1:30 in the morning.

"Gosh, Mom," Rodney had said. "It's the 2000 Olympic Torch four blocks from our house. Everybody's going to be there."

"No discussion." At home she sounded the same as she sounded at school. "You have school tomorrow. If you went out at one, you'll find, as the TV says about every place so far, the procession will be at least two hours late and by that time you'll be awake for the rest of the night. You'll sleep in class tomorrow." Having one's mother as principal of one's school was at least a double disadvantage if not a downright disability.

"Dad?" Rodney had turned to his father for a desperate but futile second opinion. Their parents always agreed on what the boys could and couldn't do. Their father shook his head sadly.

So, since the 2000 Olympic Torch being carried near their house was a once in a lifetime chance, Rodney convinced Michael it was worth another chance — of getting caught sneaking out. Besides, their upstairs bathroom window opened onto the gentle roof from which they could inch down onto the patio wall. If they set a patio chair beneath the spot before going to bed, even their final step down from the wall would be easy. As far as getting in and out of the window, they'd both seen their parents take out the screens for window washing. Easy enough.

All had gone well on their early morning sneak. Michael even took his camera and shot photos of the runner with the torch and the other runners and cars following. After the parade passed and the boys walked back toward their house, Rodney said, "You'll have to hide those pictures for nine years."

"Why?"

"Because by that time you'll be a legal adult and mom and dad can't ground you."

The way back had been smooth: Up the patio chair onto the wall, over the roof, into the bathroom window. When they stepped into the bathroom, however, the light went on. Their mother stood in her bathrobe, arms crossed. How were the boys to know that every night when their father got up to the bathroom he came upstairs to peek in on them? The front door slammed. "That's your dad. He's been out looking for you."

The boys now sat together on Rodney's bed. Anxiety and dread caught up with them as deep fatigue. But no matter how heavy their eyes felt, their mother told them to sit there until their parents returned with a verdict. The boys knew the routine. Their parents were deciding on the punishment and they wouldn't be back until they agreed exactly. When either parent mentioned a specific punishment, they did so in identical words. When it came to punishment, the parents sounded like robots — their voices monotone, listing the reasons and announcing their decision.

Their parents entered the bedroom. Michael leaned into Rodney. Their mother, clearly tired, stood straight and spoke crisply in a voice like she was announcing on the school intercom, "Boys, you disobeyed us and put yourself in danger. We —"

"We were so scared," their father rushed over and hugged them. He started to cry.

Their mother stayed by the door, hesitated, cleared her throat, and said, "Ah, boys, because —"

But their father cried even louder and hugged the boys harder. The boys cried too. "We didn't know what happened to you," their father said. "We thought somebody stole you."

"We…" their mother tried to continue, but she realized that the boys couldn't hear because their father held their heads next to him and his hands covered their ears.

However, they heard him say, "Let's not, Hon," and they were as shocked as their mother. The three males looked to the doorway where the boys' mother said, "We, ah —"

"No, let's not. Please," he said.

She blinked, then blinked again and slightly shook her head as she did when trying to get the water from her ears after swimming.

"You boys go to sleep, now," their father said. He hugged them and motioned to their mother who walked over to them with slow, stiff steps, looking confused. She hugged them too. When their parents were gone, Rodney let out a long sigh and smiled to his brother.

Michael reached over next to his bed and grabbed his camera, "You know, the map in the newspaper showed that the torch parade is going in a big circle. We could find a place tonight to see them again."

Proper 8 / Pentecost 3 / Ordinary Time 13
Matthew 10:40-42
by Craig Kelly

The Tie

This was the hardest part. One would think that after doing this so many times, it would become automatic. But he still had to talk himself through it.

"Fat end over skinny... fat end up and through... fat end — is it the fat or skinny end, now — fat, yes, fat end over to the left...."

"Come on, honey! We're going to be late, and you know there's always a huge line!"

"I know, dear, I know, just give me a minute, okay?"

She yelled again from outside the room. "You're tying that tie, aren't you?"

"No!" he yelled before thinking about it. Grimacing, he finally yelled, "Yes," although slightly quieter than before.

"Jake, you've had trouble with that Windsor knot as long as I've known you! Don't worry about it! We've got to go!" The voice was getting impatient.

"Mary, now, we've talked about this! If I'm going, I'm wearing a tie! Got it?" He grimaced again. He softened his tone while keeping the same volume. "It's important, Mary. You know how I feel about this."

Hurriedly, he turned his attention back to his bedroom mirror. Quietly, he continued: "Fat end back around to the right... back up underneath... through the loop, and —" he gave it a tug to tighten it — "done." Flipping his collar back down, he hastily reached into the closet for his suit jacket, pulling it off the metal hanger with such force that it twirled around the curtain rod like a gymnast, finally falling with a ting onto the floor, a piece of metal bent and deformed by the force of Jake's pull.

Jake took a quick look at it. I'll fix it later, he thought. At least that's something I can do.

"Coming, Mary!" He broke out into as much as a run as his bum leg could muster, although to the average onlooker, it wouldn't look like running. Ever since that cave-in at the coal mine 23 years ago that crushed the muscles in his leg, walking without a cane, let alone running, was a battle.

"Jake! Jake, don't run now! We'll have time, don't worry," Mary said as she ran as fast toward the bedroom as her high heels would let her. This, too, did not look like much of a run to the average spectator.

She met Jake at the door of their bedroom, stabilizing him just as he was about to lose balance. Holding him up, she smiled. "We have more time than I thought. We'll make it." He knew she was lying, but he didn't argue.

Their bedroom was at the end of a long corridor that ran from it past another bedroom and a bathroom, finally to the kitchen/dining room of their small trailer. Wasn't much, but it kept the rain off, as Jake would say. Handing Jake his cane, Mary took his free hand and led him down the hallway, out the front door, to their awaiting '88 Chevy truck. Just like every Thursday before, just like every Thursday to come.

After coaxing the engine back to life, Mary guided their truck down a small road, turning onto the hilly, twisting road that was West Virginia Highway 15. Jake never spoke during this particular weekly trip. Mary never spoke either, giving Jake his space. Jake just rolled down his window, allowing the mountain air to play in his salt-and-pepper hair — more salt than pepper these days. His birth certificate swore he was only 62, but he may as well have been 92. He felt that old.

Old... old and poor... old and poor and useless.... He could keep going, but that was a dark road, and he didn't feel like leading his mind down there again.

After a 25-minute drive, they finally reached their destination: Mount Sinai Mountain Mission. Grocery day. The lineup had indeed already started, trailing out the front door, down the porch steps, and past the front corner of the house. They would be waiting a while. It was usually an all-day affair anyway. Dressed in his good, black suit with his blue-striped tie, Jake slowly slipped out of the cab, leaning on his cane for balance. Mary came around, dressed in her bright blue paisley dress, walking gingerly in her high heels, extending her hand to help support her husband. Once Jake regained his bearings, they slowly made their way to the end of the line.

For as long as it was, the line was moving fairly quickly. Within an hour, they were slowly making their way up the porch steps, able to see inside the mission, where paper bags full of groceries awaited. Wouldn't be long now.

Jake hated it. Every moment of it. He never had to take handouts from anyone. Yet here he was, holding out his hand like a beggar in the street. It sickened him. That's why he had to dress up every Thursday; at least he wasn't going to look like a beggar.

One by one, each family filtered in, got their bag, and filtered out. At last, Jake and Mary made their way to the front door. Jake wondered in the back of his mind where the mission group was from this time. If he remembered correctly, Mel, the elderly man who ran the facility with his wife, Jan, said last week that the group today would be from... one of those short-named states... Ohio? Iowa? Utah? Something like that. They were all the same anyway. Come to the poor part of West Virginia, hand out some macaroni and cheese, talking about how they're the "Body of Christ," his "hands and feet" and all that, and go home feeling good about themselves. Nothing ever changes.

Just as Jake and Mary's turn was about to come up, Mel made his way out the door. A big-bellied, big-bearded man with a constant smile on his face, Mel always reminded Jake of Santa Claus, except he was there all the time with groceries instead of toys. His smile was still beaming.

"Hey, Jake, how you doing?" He placed a firm yet gentle hand on Jake's shoulder.

"Hey, Mel, doing good — you?"

"Not too bad, Jake, not too bad. Looking sharp, as always."

"Thanks, Mel. You're looking good too." Jake barely looked at him.

Mel turned his attention to the lineup. "Hey, everyone, how's it going? Just wanted to let you know that we're getting some kids from the team to work the front desk. Now, they're still learning the ropes, so be real patient with them, okay? Okay, they should be ready here to get going again in just a few minutes!" He flashed his big smile and shuffled back into the mission.

Great. Another delay. This day would never end. Jake sighed in frustration, resigned to wait his turn.

As he looked through the doorway, Jake thought he saw someone in the corner fidgeting. Finally there came a grunt of frustration.

"I can't get it!"

Jake looked to see a young member of the mission team, maybe thirteen or fourteen, struggling with something on his shirt. One of the older members of the team, a lady, came to check on the frustrated teen.

"I can't get this tie to work!" Obviously, this team placed an emphasis on formal dress. The kids had to wear ties too.

Unfortunately, the female missionary had little experience working with ties. The kid was definitely in trouble.

"Hey, you trying to use a Windsor knot?"

The kid looked up to see who was speaking. Jake was surprised to discover it was him.

"Uh, yeah," the kid replied.

Jake shuffled into the mission, working his way over to the teenage stranger. He pulled up a chair, slowly sinking into it.

"My dad tried to show me how to do it before I left, but I can't remember," the boy said sheepishly.

"Well, let's see what we can do about that," Jake said, trying to sound confident. He reached up and untied his tie, letting it hang around his neck. "Okay, kid, stand here beside me and do what I do." The boy obeyed without a word. "Now, let the fat end hang down a little lower," Jake began, pulling the boy's tie down a bit at the one end. "There you go. Now, fat end over skinny..." Jake demonstrated on his own. "Right... bring the fat end up and through the hole, like you're tying a shoelace... that's right...." Jake slowly repeated the same litany he said to himself every Thursday morning in front of the mirror. The young missionary hung on his every word, following Jake's instructions to the letter, watching the old mountain man's tie to make sure he was doing it right. "Now, pull the fat end up underneath one more time... now tuck it under that loop you made there... good. Now pull the fat end through.... There you have it! Now hold the skinny end and tighten it up." They simultaneously pulled the knot on their ties up to the collar. Jake smiled. "Not bad for a first try."

The boy beamed a wide grin as he showed off his knot-tying skills to Jake. "Thank you, sir," he said, "I'll do my best to remember how to do this. I really appreciate it."

Jake smiled a little wider. "Ah, it was nothin'," he said. Leaning on his cane, he rose to his feet, Mary was quickly at his side to steady him. Funny, his feet felt a little lighter now. The boy quickly ran behind the front counter, grabbing a bag of groceries. He slowly carried it to Mary, trying to be careful not to drop it. "Here you go, ma'am," he said politely. Mary thanked him and steadied Jake as they made their way out of the mission.

As they walked back to the truck, Mary noticed that Jake still had a smile on his face. Catching her staring, Jake grinned a little even as he struggled to hobble his way to the truck. "You doing good?" Mary asked.

"Yeah, I'm doing good," Jake replied, still smiling. "It's not every day you get the chance to teach Jesus how to tie a tie."

Proper 9 / Pentecost 4 / Ordinary Time 14
Matthew 11:16-19, 25-30
by Scott Dalgarno

What Can Brown Do for You?

Dennis Brown was Harper Elementary School's ace-in-the-hole. If there was a child who couldn't be corralled, charmed, softened, consoled, or reigned-in by him that child didn't exist. That's what people said, anyway. They said he could even put the breaks on Alberto: 48 pounds of pure Latin fire. Alberto's third-grade teacher was put on three months of administrative leave for taping him to his chair one Friday after lunch. "I broke," she said to her principal, while cleaning out her desk. It was a terrible way to treat a child, everyone agreed, but still, it was sad that it took that "train wreck" for the superintendent of schools to pony-up the money to hire a second, much-needed, special education specialist for Harper.

Dennis made the job look easy from day one. The staff was in awe of what he could do with autistic kids, pouters, fighters, and kids with ballistic tempers like Alberto. They told him he was born to it. They said they wondered how they'd gotten along without him, and then they remembered that they hadn't.

Dennis, for his part, said the job was only temporary. He thought maybe he wanted to do something else someday, but didn't know what, exactly. In the meantime, his fan club among kids and staff grew and grew. His biggest fan was Alberto, no doubt about it. On the playground, they were inseparable, and the change in Alberto was cataclysmic. It was great for everyone to see what could happen with a kid with a temper like that. It broke everyone's heart when Alberto's father brought his son into the school office one day in January, saying they would be moving on to Arizona where he had secured a job in a brand-new prison.

Alberto was inconsolable, and so was Harper Elementary. Dennis did his best to say good-bye with a smile but everyone, including Alberto, could see how hard it was for him. Dennis worried about what being a prison guard might do to Alberto's dad, and, in turn, to Alberto.

Dennis tried hard to carry on. He did his best. His circle of fans continued to grow but some of the joy had gone from working with "difficult" children. He began to think he wanted to find a job where he wouldn't have to bring the burden of his job home with him every night. He began to think he wanted a physical job where the fruits of his labors would be more tangible.

Within a month, he'd taken a job delivering packages. He wore a chocolate-colored uniform and carried an electronic clipboard with him. At first he enjoyed the work. He got lots of exercise and returned every afternoon with an empty truck. He made a little more money than he had teaching, as well, right from the start. Then his supervisor began to time him, insisting that he drive more quickly, and deliver more packages. The man didn't exactly say Dennis should take shorter lunches, but he implied it.

Dennis began to wonder if he made a mistake. He also realized that most of the packages he delivered were full of meaningless junk. At the same time, he began to miss being everyone's hero. Teaching took a toll on him, sure, but so did hustling packages all day. There were burdens both ways. Which was lighter, he wondered. He wasn't sure. It depended on the day, but he did know the answer to one question.

When he was older and looked back on his life, which job would give him the greater satisfaction? Answer: Being there for kids like Alberto. There was no doubt about that.

Some time later, on a windy-wet day in March he found himself delivering what looked like curriculum to an elementary school in neighboring, Ashville. There he got the first break he'd gotten all day, standing still, dripping in front of the principal's desk, clipboard in hand, waiting for her to get off the phone. "Where, in the name of heaven, am I going to find a certified special education teacher three months into the school year?" she shouted into the receiver. Dennis had an answer for her. Within two weeks he was back on a playground, playing dodgeball, and having the time of his life. He had a new best friend too. His name was Miguel. Miguel's eyes were darker than that big old box of a truck Dennis had driven on every street in that county, and they were glued to the tall addition to Hedrick Elementary.

Proper 10 / Pentecost 5 / Ordinary Time 15
Genesis 25:19-34
by Keith Hewitt

Taxicab Confessions

She was standing at the corner when the cab pulled up. Young, with strawberry blond hair pulled back and stuffed under a cap, wearing an oversized sweatshirt and sweatpants — an outfit no girl would choose to wear on a planet where there might be boys. Her eyes were red and puffy; in one hand was her purse, in the other a brochure that had been folded in half.

The driver sized her up through the window of her cab for a moment or two, then lowered it and leaned over and down, slightly, so she could look the girl in the eyes. "You called for a cab, Miss?"

The girl glanced down the row of houses, then back at her, pulled open the back door, and slid in. "Yeah," she agreed and closed the door with a decisive thud.

The driver raised the window, tripped the meter, checked her mirrors, and pulled out into traffic behind a bakery truck; the aroma of fresh bread snaked in through the open vents. "Where to?" she asked, looking into the rearview mirror.

"Tenth and Division."

"Tenth and Division," the driver repeated. "Doctor's appointment?" she guessed, looking in the mirror again.

"No."

"Right."

The girl lied; there was nothing there but doctors' offices, and the driver knew it. She drove quietly for a minute or two, taking in the smell from the truck, the sounds from the street, the sun flooding down and bouncing off other cars, painting the windshield with quick, sweeping swaths of glare. "Beautiful day, isn't it?" she ventured finally.

"Any chance I could just have quiet?" The girl's voice was tense.

"I guess there's always that chance."

They drove in silence for about a mile; occasionally the driver looked back at her passenger, sizing her up. Finally, she cleared her throat and said, "Summer used to be my favorite time of the year — out of school, on my own. Summer's when I met Jimmy Ray. 'Course that was twenty years ago. Before you were even born, I'll bet."

"I'm sure it's a beautiful story."

"Not so much. It was all sunshine and flowers for the first couple weeks, but then...." She trailed off, drove in silence for a ways.

"But then?" her passenger asked after a long silence, in spite of herself.

"Sorry. Then things took kind of a bad turn, I guess. You know how it is, I was in l-o-v-e," she stretched it out melodically, turned for a moment to glance over her shoulder, a sardonic smile on her face. "Convinced myself it was a love like no other. Or let Jimmy Ray convince me, I should say."

"They can do that, can't they?" the girl asked in a small voice.

The driver smiled to herself. "He sure could. Fourth of July weekend — he convinced me a couple of times, down by Red Arrow Park, and once up at the marina. On a boat." Her eyes caught her passenger's briefly, and she added, "Turned out, it wasn't his boat. And that wasn't the only thing he was — uh — less than truthful about."

She fell silent again, navigating through a knot of traffic around a pothole repair. "So what happened?" the girl asked after a minute or so.

"About what you'd expect when a kid old enough to know better sells herself cheap. By Labor Day I knew I was pregnant."

"Oh." She didn't say it, but it was the purse of her lips, the knowing look in her eyes.

"Yup. Took two of those tests and a visit to the doctor to convince me. I tried to get Jimmy Ray to come to the doctor with me, but all of a sudden, he wasn't calling me back. By the time I got up the courage to go over there, his phone was disconnected and he was gone."

"What did you do?"

"Well, I'd like to tell you that I went home, told my folks, and we sat down as a family to look at all the options."

"You did?"

"No. That's what I'd like to tell you. Truth was, I was scared spitless. Here I was, just starting school again, and all I could think of was how hard it was going to be. I looked ahead, and all I saw was 99 miles of bad road. And my folks — I couldn't tell my folks. I might as well have just gone ahead and told 'em I was going to vote Republican in the next election — that would have killed 'em just as dead."

They were at a light; she fell silent again, for a heartbeat or two, closed her eyes and felt herself being tugged back there — the fear, the hopelessness, the anger mixed with panic, they all flooded back to her. She opened her eyes, took a deep breath, then another. "Funny thing," she said, "sometimes to get what you think you want in the present, you end up giving away the future. And, sweetheart, that's just way too expensive."

"I think I see what you mean," the girl said. Her eyes held the driver's now. "What happened?"

She shrugged. "I was young, I had plans. All I saw was my life being ruined. So I figured the only way I could get it back was to trade — a life for a life. It just made sense." She started to slow, as they neared Tenth and Division. "And not a day goes by — not a day — when I wonder if I made the right decision."

"Do you have children now?" the girl asked, suddenly wanting to direct this woman away from her thoughts, the pain she saw in her eyes, and the way she gripped the wheel.

The driver nodded, relaxed a little as she slid the car into a spot in front of the Medical Arts Building and put it in park. She opened the glove compartment, pulled out a wallet and turned in her seat, unsnapping the wallet as she turned. It fell open, and she held it apart with one hand, flipped through the vinyl photo holder with the other. The first sleeve was empty, she folded it up and out of the way, tapped the second one with a fingertip. "My boys. Twins, eight years old." She flipped them up after the girl nodded, to the next sleeved. "My dog, Brutus. He's a Lab-Rotweiller mix. Dumb as a post, but all heart." The girl smiled, nodded, and she flipped to the next picture. "My husband — 41 going on 12. He's great. They're all great."

"So it's worked out for you?"

"I guess," she agreed and started to close the wallet.

"What about the first one?" the girl asked. "Picture fall out?"

"No," the driver said, pausing for a moment to look at the empty sleeve, then pulled the wallet back, laid it on the seat next to her. "That one's empty. It always will be."

The young girl looked puzzled for a moment, then her eyes fell. "Oh," she half-whispered.

As the girl paid and slipped out of the car, the driver said nothing. Once she was out and standing uncertainly on the sidewalk, the driver rolled the window down once again, and leaned over. "Good luck, Miss," she said earnestly. "God bless you."

"You too," the girl said, fingering the brochure in her hand.

"Oh, he does — no matter how hard I make it for him, he does. He loves me, you know. And he loves you too." The girl smiled uncertainly; the driver rolled up the window and pulled away slowly, one finger still rubbing softly over the empty picture sleeve.

As she looked in the mirror, the girl stepped down off the curb and raised her hand to hail a cab....

Proper 11 / Pentecost 6 / Ordinary Time 16
Genesis 28:10-19a
by Argile Smith

The Land's Sacred

Walter had been a farmer almost all of his life. He grew up in a sharecropper's home where he, his parents, and his two younger brothers worked in the field day in and day out. When he left home at the age of eighteen, he vowed that he would never return to the farm. After a couple of years away, however, he started to miss the dirt, the seeds, the tractor, and the possibility of seeing something come up out of the ground. So he decided to go back to the soil. For the rest of his life, he worked the land as a farmer.

At first, the land he worked didn't belong to him. He rented it from a real estate mogul named Austin who had bought a huge tract of land so he could sell it later and make a big profit. A few years earlier, Austin had inherited his father's fortune. He also inherited his dad's knack for making money. However, he lacked one instinct that Walter possessed: an intuition for the real value of land.

For seven years Walter rented a small corner of Austin's parcel of land. During that time, he saved enough money to make a down payment on the property he had been renting. He hoped that Austin would sell it to him one day.

When he thought the time had come to talk with Austin about buying the land he had been working, Walter took a deep breath, picked up the phone at his house, and called his landlord. Of course, he had to wade through a pool of assistants, but he remained patient until he heard Austin's voice on the other end of the line.

"Walter, I'm glad you called," Austin said with a hint of pleasure in his voice. He always enjoyed his conversations with Walter, even though they rarely lasted longer than a few minutes.

"Well, Austin, thanks for talking with me."

"What can I do for you?"

"I'll get right to the point. I want you to sell me the land that I've been renting from you."

For a second or two, Austin said nothing, nothing at all. Silence on the other end of the line gave Walter a clue that what he had just said may not have set well with Austin. He knew that his landlord didn't want to break up his huge tract of land into small parcels. The silence could only mean that Austin's mind was sorting through his request, processing it with a view toward the best way to make the biggest profit.

Austin broke the silence with a comment meant to discourage Walter. "You can't afford that land," he warned.

Walter countered, "Yes I can. I've already talked to the bank about it. I can get the money, and I know that I can make the payments."

"Why do you want to burden yourself with a mortgage? Just keep on renting the land."

"Because one day you're going to sell it, and I want to hold on to it and pass it along to my nephew after I'm gone."

"That's an awfully big risk to take just to have some old farm land," Austin said.

"For you, it's just old farm land. For me, it's more than that. It's something sort of sacred," Walter explained. He went on to say that when he worked the land through planting season and harvest time, he sensed something special about the ground and the crops that came from it. He sensed God's presence as he worked in the field. That's why it meant something more to him than an investment. It was a sacred place that he wanted to preserve.

Of course, Austin couldn't refuse Walter's request, even though he tried at first. Just like Walter said, Austin sold the rest of the property later on to a group of developers. For him, land was an investment. For Walter, land was something else. Somehow, it was sacred.

God promised Jacob that he would bring him back to the land of Israel (Genesis 28:15). Paul said that God will redeem the land when he comes for his children (Romans 8:21). The earth on which we live is part of God's great creation that he considers special.

Proper 12 / Pentecost 7 / Ordinary Time 17
Romans 8:26-39
by David O. Bales

Never Again Separate

Ellie made it from the basement parking lot into the elevator and up to the eighth floor without thinking it yet. She passed a crash cart and walked by an open door where she concluded that someone needed to help a patient off the commode soon. She turned right into another hall and saw the nurses' station ahead. Still, by a masterful exercise of her mind, she pushed the thought away. However, when she saw the RN's head bent down, probably charting a patient, she could no longer keep the thought at bay: I wonder if Tate has died yet?

Maybe, she wondered, when I've been a chaplain for eighteen years instead of nine, I'll be able to protect myself from pain longer. I'll delay the onset of consciousness longer. Maybe I'll stop hurting the moment I step from a patient's room and not hurt until I enter again.

She thought now about Tate, no putting off the pain anymore. She leaned against the counter. The nurse's head was still down. "Betty," Ellie said, "how's Reverend Tate in 21?"

"Ah, let me look. He was Johnson's last night." She shuffled and flipped a few papers, then looked on both sides of her. "There it is." She grabbed a chart and handed it to Ellie. That answered her question. He was still alive.

She instantly turned and followed her training if not her instincts. Do the hardest first. Reverend Tate was the hardest. He'd gotten her into this. He was her pastor ten years ago: Reverend Tate the straightest and most moral arrow ever shot at a congregation. Also the most frustrating and maddening. But he'd discerned Ellie's gifts and potential and encouraged her to become a hospital chaplain.

She rounded the last corner and saw Nurse Johnson coming. Johnson knew what Ellie was going through. As they passed, Johnson reached over and brushed Ellie's shoulder with her hand, grimaced, and said, "He's alive."

He'd lived until Tuesday as Ellie feared he would. This would be the day of the meeting. Ellie took a stutter step, grit her teeth, and turned into 821.

"Ham coming?" was the first thing Reverend Tate said, having turned his head toward Ellie.

"He's coming," she said.

"I'll wait," he said and closed his eyes.

Hamilton Pritchard was the congregation's associate pastor when the congregation asked Reverend Tate to retire at seventy. Pritchard stayed on as senior pastor. Since he retired Reverend Tate had never gone back to the congregation nor spoken with Hamilton Pritchard. Publicly he said he remained away in order to give the current pastors "a free hand" in ministry. Ellie, in the confidentiality of serving as hospital chaplain, heard all about his anger and anguish. After his retirement a series of illnesses regularly brought him to the hospital. Now he was dying.

Ellie had phoned Hamilton Pritchard at a denominational meeting Monday evening, telling him of Tate's illness and that Tate wanted to see him. Pritchard said he'd fly home and be to the hospital by morning.

Ellie wouldn't talk with Tate now. She knew he was saving his strength to talk with Hamilton Pritchard. Would his eight years of silent suffering emerge as anger to Pritchard? She stood in the hall, back straight against the wall and prayed.

"Ellie." It was Hamilton Pritchard. He looked tired but concerned. "You okay?"

"Yeah, well, worried about Tate."

"How is he?"

"Alive and he wants to talk to you."

"Eight years," he looked down and shook his head. "I don't think there's been a day I haven't prayed for him. But I'm still scared to face him."

In Ellie's job people immediately told her the truth. As she watched Hamilton Pritchard enter room 821, she prayed that Tate and Pritchard could speak the truth to one another in love.

* * *

A week later Hamilton Pritchard requested that Ellie read scripture at Reverend Tate's funeral. The order of worship placed the scripture after the sermon.

The sanctuary was half full, many of the new members not having known Reverend Tate. The service was simple. The congregation sang two hymns. Three colleagues of Tate spoke for five minutes each — all mentioning how important it was for Tate to do the right thing and above all not to hurt anyone.

Then Reverend Pritchard spoke. "For Nathan Tate this congregation was his family, from which he expected too much. Nathan and I talked about it two days before he died. This congregation wasn't morally perfect in its dealing with an aging pastor. He wasn't morally upright in his response, remaining, as he said, in exile from the congregation.

"But none of us always understands what is ethically required of us and none of us lives in a morally perfect way. If we did, we wouldn't need a Savior.

"Nathan Tate asked me to apologize to you for his eight years of separation. He also asked that a portion of the eighth chapter of Paul's letter to the Romans be read. This text explains our Christian hope and the one solution for our problems in or out of the church."

When he sat, Ellie approached the pulpit. She couldn't push away her pain, yet she could say something deeply true, "Add me to the list of those who hope and pray for the final reunion Paul promises, 'For I am convinced that neither death, nor life, nor angels, nor rulers, nor things present, nor things to come, nor powers, nor height, nor depth, nor anything else in all creation, will be able to separate us from the love of God in Christ Jesus our Lord.' "

Proper 13 / Pentecost 8 / Ordinary Time 18
Matthew 14:13-21; Psalm 17:1-7, 15
by Argile Smith

Compassion at Work

George had the good fortune to make plenty of money in the first half of his life. He had a knack for business and he didn't mind working hard. Having been raised in near poverty, he knew about being hungry, sick, and poor. Somewhere along the way toward adulthood, he climbed over the wall of his oppressive situation and made something valuable of himself. He was the quintessential self-made man.

But as the second half of his life rolled around, he lost interest in building an empire. Instead, he turned his attention to putting his money to work so other people could climb over the wall to a better life. Developing a foundation through which he could carry out his work, he set out to give away much of his wealth to causes that would help people break out of poverty.

One day he received a letter from a man named Les who needed some help. In the letter, Les shared the sad story of his daughter who had been diagnosed with a rare form of cancer. The disease had taken almost all of her childhood and left her in almost constant agony. The treatments to cure her had taken a terrible toll on her body and, of course, on the family checkbook. Les elaborated that the previous Christmas had been meager for his daughter because most of their resources had to be spent on his little girl's medical care. He ended the letter with a plea for help.

Something about the letter captured George's attention and gripped his heart. Perhaps he hadn't read a letter like it in a while, or maybe he recalled the number of Christmas trees he had seen in his house when he was little boy that had no presents under them. The more he read the letter about Les' daughter, the more something inside him moved him to pull out his own checkbook and write a check for a generous amount to help her and her family. Then he instructed his assistant to mail the check to the return address on the envelope that contained Les' letter to him.

Months passed and George hadn't heard anything from Les about his daughter's situation. Even though George had plenty of initiatives to occupy his attention, he still couldn't get the little girl and her poor health off his mind. One day he decided to find out how she was doing, so he asked his assistant to get some updated information on her condition.

After a few hours, his assistant finished the investigation and gave George a disappointing report. After investigating the matter, George's assistant had discovered that everything Les had said about his daughter was a total lie. Although Les lived at the address indicated on the return address of the envelope, he didn't have a daughter who was sick. In fact, he didn't have a daughter at all. He lived by himself.

George had been taken by a slick con artist. His assistant reported that Les had a history of scamming people like George out of money. Although he had been caught a couple of times, he always managed to weasel his way past the legal system. The gift George sent had been spent all right, but not to care for a sick child.

After George heard the report, he sat in silence for a moment. And then he said, "I'm glad that the little girl doesn't really have cancer." Then he thanked his assistant for helping him and went on with his work.

Jesus fed 5,000 people because he felt compassion for them (Matthew 14:14). The psalmist asked God to show his loving kindness — or compassion (Psalm 7:7). Compassion comes from God's heart, and it flows into his people who share his heart.

Proper 14 / Pentecost 9 / Ordinary Time 19
Matthew 14:22-33
by David O. Bales

Out of the Same Boat With Peter

The old man shook his head as though to clear his thinking. He looked down at a dozen anxious, starving people sitting around him on the floor of the house in Jerusalem. They stared at the old man eagerly. They heard Judean soldiers on the street yelling and running outside the house. "Forty years later," the old man said to the group, "the story of Jesus and Peter on the lake can seem so simple — crisp, clean, and obvious. And I've heard people mutter that Peter was a coward or, worse, that he had no faith."

The old man, wobbling from hunger, looked compassionately on each of these trembling Christians. "Peter got out of the boat in the worst of it. Remember that. Those who don't pity Peter are like young men eager to be soldiers who've never seen war. Peter stepped out of the boat onto the roughest of seas, trusting the Lord toward whom he walked. We servants of Jesus don't tell you of Peter and Jesus on Galilee's lake so you can congratulate yourselves, thinking, 'Well, I wouldn't have worried about the wind as Peter. I'd have trusted my Lord.' If anyone is going to scold Peter, let it be only his Lord Jesus who loved him and saved him. Trust my lifetime of living for Jesus when I urge you not to concentrate on Peter's faltering. Instead, remember Jesus' reaching out and saving him."

More yelling comes from the street outside: "The Romans are over the north wall."

"Not many boats up here in the hills," he smiled feebly. "Any of you even seen a boat?" Two people nodded that they had seen a boat. Some others of the group might have gazed upon a boat but were too numbed by fear to respond. Most everyone held tightly to the persons sitting beside them. "Well, makes no difference that most of Jesus' students in Galilee were used to boats and a bunch of us were fishermen. That evening we'd left Jesus to pray by himself and we started across the lake. Shouldn't have taken long but that storm fell on the lake and tormented us head-on with waves."

Somewhere not far away a man's high voice repeated a shriek, "They got through the temple and their slaughtering the priests." Muffled yells answered him. The sandals of many people pounded quickly past the house.

The huddled Christians tried to listen to the old man, no matter the destruction that so obviously approached them. "On the little mast the ropes pulled as tight as harp strings and the wind played an eerie melody on them. The sail yanked away like a rug being shaken in the morning's cleaning."

Outside the house the crowd, running by, crashed against the door, causing everyone to cower. A young couple whimpered.

"We were in peril of our lives. You'd have been as terrified as we were. The storm made the night completely black. We bumped into the fellow next to us as we scrambled to row or bail or right the boat. Lightning flashed and instantly lit up our desperation like a gigantic lamp; then, darkness enveloped us again, even darker, as the thunder crushed us."

The people listening to the old man smelled smoke and then heard the crackling and snapping of a growing fire. The old man sighed, "The early dawn, just before Jesus came, was the worst. We were exhausted from bailing, couldn't scoop water any faster. We had, right then, lost the battle against the storm. We'd given up hope and, as the last splashes came over the boat's side, we stopped trying because the water poured in. Let me say, that's when you most need faith in life beyond this world."

At the sound of a child's cry outside everyone looked toward the door. The old man tottered but continued, "God's love in Jesus was hard to believe then, as it is hard to believe now. Nature's storm or the storm of Romans ruining all of Judea — same destruction, same terror. I've told you before about Jesus' resurrection. Don't forget that first was his crucifixion, like a cyclone of hatred swallowing him. Let me assure you," he said as they heard swords clashing outside the house, "if you see the wind, as Peter did, and you're frightened, God doesn't reject you for that. Then as now..."

Roman soldiers were crashing against the door. Everyone cringed. The old man looked to the door. With one hand he motioned for his listeners to do as he did. Then he extended the other hand toward the door. Roman soldiers charged in. He quickly repeated, "Then as now..." The last thing he said was, "In life's storms, we have to trust Jesus to reach out to us — in this life or the next."

Proper 15 / Pentecost 10 / Ordinary Time 20
Romans 11:1-2a, 29-32
by C. David McKirachan

You're Stuck

I was a student at San Francisco Theological Seminary and the Graduate Theological Union. It was a wonderful environment for study, contemplation, and discovery. It was a great place for asking questions. I encountered ideas, ideals, visions, theological juxtaposition, metaphysical plurality, and other things that we won't discuss at the moment.

I had always been a bit liberal. In my family it was hard not to. We were taught that the gospel was intended to liberate people. We were big on the prophets. We were also taught that if you were going to try to teach the love of Christ to someone, you'd better give two hoots about their well-being on any level that was needful. For some the kingdom of God is a bowl of rice or a job. We were taught that we all have a call but every call is based on the compassion and justice of the Lord. So, with my father preaching and my mother prodding, it was kind of hard to avoid a ministry of involvement with the poor.

With years at a northeastern private college behind me and the lights of San Francisco twinkling through fog rolling through the Golden Gate in front of me, the poor were a social construct, a theoretical demographic, a Hebrew and a Greek word to be wrestled into place. I had discussions about these theories but that's about how deep it got. I was in the wading pool of ethical involvement.

I went over to the city once in a while. There were things in San Fran that Berkeley and San Anselmo lacked. I took the bus when I could. It was cheaper than parking and I enjoyed walking up and down the hills. Coming home one evening, I waited in a bus garage with a few others. There were no amenities. It was a place where buses pulled in as they disgorged and ingested passengers. Standing away from the bunch was a scruffy individual. He wobbled even when he leaned against a pillar. Then he turned, leaning on the upright and vomited on the floor. It went on for a while. The bunch turned away. It stank in the enclosed space. It smelled of whiskey among other things. I went over to him. I felt sorry for the poor guy.

"Do you need some help? Is there anything I can do?"

He turned to me, ruined teeth and blood shot eyes, bleary with the booze and the sickness and he told me that it would be a big help if I did something to myself. He said it with such vehemence that he lost his balance. Reflexively I grabbed his arm. He steadied and then took a swing at me. I was young and he was drunk. He missed. But I got the message. I retreated.

The punch had not landed, but there was a pain in my gut that felt as if it had. He radiated pain. He was a mess. I wanted to help. He hated me. I couldn't deal with the amount of hopelessness and living horror that stalked there. I said a prayer. It was a selfish prayer. "Please Lord, I'll go anywhere. Just don't send me to the city. I can't stand the pain."

Five years later, I sat with my father discussing a congregation's invitation to me to be their pastor. He listened to my enthusiasm and my reservations. Then he reminded me of my encounter with the drunk in the bus station. "Can you stand the pain?" I was amazed. I had forgotten. He had remembered my emotions and my selfish prayer. Honestly, I said, "I don't know." Then he asked me, "Do you feel called?" All the theoretical and philosophic justifications fell away. All the ideals and enthusiasms seemed small. Those two questions ran head-on into each other and demanded that I make a choice. I sat quiet, stuck.

He said very quietly, "David, when I thought I couldn't stand the pain, I remembered the Lord. He felt the same way. But he held on and went ahead with what needed doing. I guess that's what it means to be called. God gave us the gifts. Once God's involved, we're stuck."

During the years I spent in Newark, I remembered my prayer in the bus station. I remembered the insight of my father. I remembered the Lord. I thanked God for the gifts and for the call.

But I do think God has a very weird sense of humor.

Proper 16 / Pentecost 11 / Ordinary Time 21
Romans 12:1-8
by Craig Kelly

A Rose and a Scarf

The plain pine box sat silent in the parlor. One red rose was placed on top. Since there had been no viewing, it had been decided that the lid on the casket would remain closed.

Five rows of five chairs were set up to accommodate mourners, but only half of them were filled. The only ones who came were a few distant relatives, a couple of neighbors, three or four from her church, and a couple of elderly ladies traveling the "funeral circuit"; apparently they had nothing better to do.

There was no decoration, only a few floral arrangements that belonged to the funeral home. Two standing lamps cast a soft glow on the casket, one at the head and one at the foot. Soft instrumental music played "In The Garden" over the embedded speakers in the ceiling.

As the music softened, the pastor entered the room through a backdoor, dressed in a plain white robe with a black stole hanging over the shoulders, carrying a large cardboard box, taped with masking tape, in front of him. He silently walked to the podium, setting the box down behind him. He cleared his throat.

"Thank you all for coming. As you know, today we are gathered to remember and celebrate the life of Althea May James. Let us pray."

After opening in a word of prayer, the pastor continued, "I'll try not to take too long today. From the conversations I had with Althea prior to her death, I know she wouldn't want a lot of fuss and big speeches. I'm going to read you a passage of scripture not necessarily heard much at funerals, but one that I believe is appropriate for today. In Romans, Paul says, 'I appeal to you therefore, brothers, by the mercies of God, to present your bodies as a living sacrifice, holy and acceptable to God, which is your spiritual worship. Do not be conformed to this world, but be transformed by the renewal of your mind, that by testing you may discern what is the will of God, what is good and acceptable and perfect.'

"Althea May James probably lived out this scripture better than anyone I ever knew. She didn't live it loudly, but her life was a sacrifice poured out to God, even though we couldn't see it.

"You know, it says later in that passage from Romans that because we are all members of the Body of Christ, we should exercise our gifts, each as God gave us. Just as some functions of the body are less visible than others, so it is in the Body of Christ. Some of the greatest gifts God gives us get the least attention.

"Many people didn't know Althea, even people in the church she attended for so many years. She always slipped in quietly during the first hymn, sitting in the back corner of the church. She was always the first one out, and as her health declined, she had to leave earlier and earlier so she could slip out unnoticed. She always dressed clean but plain. Anyone seeing her would probably have thought she was just another poor person from the inner city, maybe a homeless woman come to find some shelter or maybe a handout.

"I myself didn't even know much about her for the first few years I was here. It was only over time that I began to see past the surface, past the quiet exterior. Over time, I began to get to know a woman of deep prayer, a woman of generous spirit, a woman of profound humility. Only a handful of us ever saw her worn and tattered Bible, with a copy of the parish directory inside. None of us heard the constant prayers she offered up to God for each family in her congregation. She knew hardly anything about them; yet their names were constantly on her lips, asking God for their welfare and preservation.

"Only a handful of us saw the socks, the scarves, the hats she knitted over and over again, her gnarled, arthritic hands wincing in pain as she worked the knitting needles. Yet, she continued in her work, not for herself, but for the homeless at the local soup kitchen, as well as for orphans in Russia and the Ukraine."

The pastor stopped for a moment, then reached behind him, cutting the tape on top of the cardboard box with his fingernail. Opening the box, he pulled out a thick woolen scarf, woven together with various shades of red and purple yarn, and then turned back to the mourners.

"Althea was even able to finish one more box of scarves and hats before she died. She never stopped working, even as the cancer continued to ravage her body. She was determined to see her calling through to the end.

"It wasn't until just before she died that I learned she had taken her life savings, everything except for a small amount to cover — barely — the funeral and burial expenses, and gave it all to aid in programs helping the homeless and destitute in this city. I remember one of the last times I visited her. I asked her why she didn't want to use more of her money to make for a better funeral or to make her more comfortable in her final days. She just smiled and said, 'Pastor, why on earth would I want to hold on to a meager treasure down here when I won't be here to use them? I want to see that they're put to good use. Besides, I'll have everything I need when I get to the other side.' Everything was so simple for her, and yet her simplicity bred a wisdom that few of us could hope to attain.

"She never looked for accolades. She never looked for worldly esteem. She was not conformed to this world but in her simple, powerful faith, she always walked in the will of God — his perfect, acceptable will.

"In a hundred years, maybe even a hundred days, no one will remember the name Althea May James. Yet, in her own quiet way, she took the gifts God gave her and used them, and her actions, though unseen here, will echo throughout eternity."

The pastor paused, swallowing hard. "If there is one thing Althea would want you to know, I think it would be this: We all have a part to play. We all have a job to do. It may be a big part that everyone sees. It may be a part that gets noticed. Or you may have a job like Althea's. You may be called to just be in the background, being faithful in the little jobs that God gives you to do. Yet whatever your job, large or small, do it with everything that is in you. If you are called to preach, preach with everything in you. If your job is to sweep floors, do it with everything in you, offering your job, yourself, as a sacrifice to the God who made you and loves you. When you have finished the race, when you have played your part, you too will hear those words: 'Well done, good and faithful servant. You have been faithful over a little; I will set you over much. Enter into the joy of your master.'"

The pastor quietly stepped away from the podium, walking over to the pine casket. He slowly placed the scarf on the coffin lid next to the rose, the shades of red and purple complimenting the deep red hue of the flower. "This was Althea May James' legacy," the pastor finally said. "She lived her calling, praying in secret and knitting scarves. I think her prayer would be — and I know mine is — that you too would dedicate yourself to drawing closer to God and following his will. Become a living sacrifice, even if all you have to show for it at the end is a rose and a scarf. It will be enough."

Proper 17 / Pentecost 12 / Ordinary Time 22
Psalm 105:1-6, 23-26, 45c
by Peter Andrew Smith

A Reason to Tell

"I'm going out," Tom said as he got up from the table. "I promised to meet the guys downtown."

"Do you have to?" Sue asked. "Uncle Stan is coming over for a visit and I was hoping you might stay home tonight."

"All that old man is going to do is tell the same old story about how he was a drunk, got stabbed in a bar fight, and how God changed his life forever." Tom rolled his eyes. "I've heard it all before."

"But maybe his story —"

"It has nothing to do with me," Tom said putting on his jacket and grabbing his car keys and wallet from the counter. "Don't wait up."

"At least promise me you won't try to drive home again," Sue said.

"I never drink that much," Tom snapped. The doorbell rang and Tom opened the door for his elderly uncle.

"I can't stay, Stan," Tom said. "I'm on my way out. Some friends are expecting me downtown."

"I see," Stan replied. "Those friends the same ones who left you passed out last month on a bench when it started to rain?"

"It wasn't that bad. They were just having fun with me."

"Sure and friends like that left me for dead outside a bar when that guy stuck me with a knife."

"Not the same thing." Tom looked at his watch. "I gotta go."

Stan grabbed Tom by the arm and locked eyes with him. "I was just like you. Going out every night to party and getting drunk with people I thought were my friends. When they left me for dead, I thought my life was over. But that night in the alley, I learned that God is faithful. He was with me when everyone else ran. He was there when the paramedics came. He got me through the long process of drying out and he's helped keep me sober ever since. He could do the same for you. All it takes is for you to accept what he offers and live a different life."

Tom shook his head. "I like my life the way it is and I want to go out."

Stan let go of his arm. "Heaven knows I can't stop you."

"That's right," Tom said straightening his jacket.

"Heaven also knows I won't stop praying for you."

Tom stopped halfway out the door. "You pray for me?"

"Sure. I pray that you come to know God and don't end up bleeding in an alley somewhere. I was wild when I was your age but it was only me." Stan pointed at Sue. "You've got a wife and family."

"Nothing's going to happen to me," Tom said as he slammed the door.

"Sorry about that, Uncle Stan," Sue said as she took his coat. "I guess you wasted your time."

"Remembering how God was good to me is never a waste of time. The story is as important for me to hear as it is for anyone else who will listen."

Sue slumped in her chair. "I don't think Tom will ever listen."

"He heard what I was saying even if he didn't like it."

"Will it make a difference?" she asked.

"I pray it does," Stan answered. "Each and every time I get a chance to remind Tom of how God has made things better in my life, I pray it brings him a step closer to knowing God himself."

Proper 18 / Pentecost 13 / Ordinary Time 23
Matthew 18:15-20
by Craig Kelly

Gathered in My Name

It had started out as a great day. The Tigers played a great game, their starter pitching a complete game shutout against the White Sox. As part of a day out with the grandkids, they wandered through the ballpark, taking in the baseball museum, riding the Ferris wheel, and enjoying a coney dog or two. All in all, a great day.

He was walking with his grandsons beside Ford Field, their Tigers pennants still being waved around in the air. Obviously they hadn't come down from their high of seeing an actual Major League Baseball game yet.

And then, as they approached the parking garage....

He first noticed the pain and tightness in his chest. Then his vision started to blur. He couldn't breathe. He thought he felt his knees hit the pavement. As he blacked out, he felt himself falling forward.

He never felt the impact of the pavement.

* * *

"We managed to get his heart beating again. However, your father's brain was deprived of oxygen," the doctor said sadly. "He's slipped into a coma. I wish I could say he'll come out of it, but experience has shown me that patients in his condition very rarely recover."

Tears streamed down her face as she held her son close to her. As soon as he had seen his grandfather collapse, he had grabbed his grandfather's cell phone and dialed 911. Even as quickly as the paramedics had arrived, it had appeared the damage had been done. He had a deathly pallor about him as he lay motionless in the hospital bed.

"What are we gonna do, Mom? Is Grandpa gonna be okay?" the younger child asked.

"I don't know, baby," his mom replied. "We've got to pray." She knelt down, wiped the tears from her eyes, and looked her son in his face. "Can you pray for Grandpa?"

The boy silently nodded, still holding his pennant.

* * *

Dear Lord, I pray right now for my father. God, they're saying it doesn't look good. I don't know what else to do but I come to you and plead for him right now. Please touch his body. Help him to open his eyes and see us and talk to us again. Lord, he loves you so much, and I know you love him too. Please, God, in Jesus' name, help him.

* * *

God, I pray for my friend's dad. I know what it's like to lose a father to a heart attack, and I pray that he will recover and she'll be spared that pain. Lord, I know you're bigger than doctor's reports, and you're bigger than sickness itself. Please touch him now, Lord, and help him to live out all his days. In Jesus' name, amen.

* * *

Dear heavenly Father, I pray for the patient in 7B23 right now. After spending time with that man's family, I know that this is a man who loves you very much, as does his family. I see so much death here in pastoral care and I know that all life is in your hands, but I pray that you would let this family see your healing power displayed in this man that it would be a testimony to all that know him. I pray that you would be glorified in this man's life even more. In Christ's name, Amen.

* * *

Dear Father, I pray for George, that you would minister to his body and heal him, in Jesus' name. He's been a wonderful neighbor and an even better witness for you all the years that I've known him. Forgive me for not taking the time to talk with him more. I know he's an amazing man of God, and I know your eye is continually on him. You love him with an everlasting love, and I pray that you would show that love in his life by healing his body right now. Let there be no brain damage, in Jesus' name. I thank you for what you're doing and what you're going to do. In Jesus' name, Amen.

* * *

God, please heal Grandpa and help him to wake up and not be sick anymore. Amen.

* * *

The eye flicker was so faint, it was hard to see it at first. The soft groan was what first got everyone's attention. Slowly, his eyelid raised showing eyes that no one had seen for three days.

"Dad? Dad, can you hear me?"

More groans.

"Dad, it's Jamie. Can you hear me?"

Another groan. Finally, words started coming out, soft and raspy. "Jamie?... The kids... the kids okay?"

Jamie covered her mouth, stifling the ecstatic scream that wanted to burst out of her mouth. "They're... they're fine," she managed to say. "I've got to let someone know." Hurriedly she ran from the room. "Doctor! Doctor!"

The youngest of the two Tigers fans pulled a chair up to the side of the bed and then climbed on it, allowing him to look his grandfather in the face.

"Grandpa? You okay?"

George's eyes started to come into focus. His mouth curled into a small smile seeing his grandson. His voice was still weak, but he managed to speak.

"How 'bout... that pitcher for the Tigers?"

Proper 19 / Pentecost 14 / Ordinary Time 24
Exodus 14:19-31
by Frank Ramirez

The Unsecret Weapon

We're all familiar with the concept of a secret weapon. Basically, it's a weapon that's kept secret from the enemy. Because they don't know what it is, they're not able to mount an adequate defense.

Of course, once such a weapon is used, it can only remain a secret for so long. The Manhattan Project, which produced the first atomic weapons, is a good example. As long as the atomic bomb was not used, it was not duplicated. No one knew it existed. But once the weapons were used in war it was only a matter of time before first one, then several other nations figured out how to build these terrible weapons. They are very dangerous, but they are not secret.

Some secret weapons don't have near the effect the builders planned. The Germans during World War II hinted they had secret weapons that would turn the tide. They produced an unpiloted aircraft that was basically a bomb with wings called the V-1. They also produced the world's first true rocket, which was labeled the V-2. They were terrible weapons, designed to demoralize the British people, but they'd already shown their courage many times during the war, and neither weapon, though they killed many hundreds, was able to create the terror the Germans had hoped would turn the tide of the war.

What about a real secret weapon, one swift and terrible, which remained a secret? The writer Isaac Asimov wrote an essay called "The Unsecret Weapon" in which he described a true secret weapon known as Greek fire. It was used by the defenders of Constantinople against the Muslims in the year 672 AD. To this day, no one knows what chemicals it contained, although it probably included a mixture of sulfur, naphtha, quicklime, and niter. When ships clogged the harbor the mixture was shot over the water. When mixed with water it caught on fire and drifted toward the ships, causing them to catch fire and creating panic. It was used several times to defend the city, and then the formula must have been lost because two centuries later it was only a legendary substance.

In that article, Asimov mentioned that a secret weapon is one thing, but what about an Unsecret Weapon? What about a weapon that was tremendously powerful, but not a secret, yet which the other side refused to use?

The English during the thirteenth and fourteenth centuries had such an Unsecret Weapon. It was called the Long Bow. Six feet in length, it was the most powerful weapon of the era. An arrow shot by such a bow could pierce armor. Thousands of bowmen could fill the sky with whizzing death, the horrifying noise of the arrows presaging the descent of doom.

On more than one occasion, the English used this well-known weapon against the French army and obliterated their foes despite the fact that they were outnumbered and on foreign soil. How could they use this Unsecret Weapon to their advantage?

There were two crucial facts about the Long Bow that made it impossible for the French to use. It took special training and it took great strength. These were qualities the nobility might not have. The idea that a commoner might be more important than a knight on a horse was impossible for the French, with their notions of blue blood. Moreover, once trained a large peasant suddenly became valuable and difficult to replace. Once again, this offended the sensibilities of the nobility.

William Shakespeare, in his play *Henry V*, wrote about the battles fought against the French with the Long Bow. He describes the morning before the Battle of Agincourt. The English are sick and starving and outnumbered five to one. The French are wagering how many they will kill before lunchtime. One character, named Westmoreland, laments,

> O that we now had here
> But one ten thousand of those men in England
> That do no work to-day!

And King Henry replies (or at least Shakespeare has him say):

> What's he that wishes so?
> My cousin Westmoreland? No, my fair cousin:
> If we are mark'd to die, we are enow
> To do our country loss; and if to live,
> The fewer men, the greater share of honour.
> God's will! I pray thee, wish not one man more.

Good King Henry then describes how in the future those who survive the battle will remember its anniversary, which was St. Crispin's Day, and that they would show off their scars and brag about it. Each year the story would come alive:

> This story shall the good man teach his son;
> And Crispin Crispian shall ne'er go by,
> From this day to the ending of the world,
> But we in it shall be remember'd;
> We few, we happy few, we band of brothers;

It's one of the grandest speeches in literature. Later, when the English vanquish the French, losing almost none of their own while killing 10,000 of the enemy, Shakespeare makes sure that his King Henry gives God all the credit. The

French themselves agree, insisting God must have wanted it that way. But truth be told, it had more to do with the Long Bow, the Unsecret Weapon, and the strong arms of the yeoman who pulled back the string.

Surely by the time God's people were led by Moses to the shore of the Red Sea, both they and Pharaoh, who was madly pursuing them, should have remembered they, too, had an Unsecret Weapon. Plagues of frogs, rivers of blood, an Angel of Death who passed over only those houses protected by the blood of a lamb — weren't these things obvious enough to anyone? Could it have been a secret to anyone that Moses served a living God?

Proper 20 / Pentecost 15 / Ordinary Time 25
Exodus 16:2-15; Philippians 1:21-30
by Argile Smith

Kristin's Faith

Landon had considered himself fortunate because he could do his work at home. With his office in his house, he had the joyful privilege of being around his daughter, Kristin. He enjoyed her dropping by and checking on him throughout the day.

Of course, she had her dad wrapped around her little finger. Her four-year-old smile captivated him more each day, so he could never tell her that he was too busy for one of her spontaneous chats. No matter how much work he had to do, conversations with her always served as the highlight of his daily routine.

In due time, however, her visits became a little too frequent. She became a little too eager to talk to her dad while he tried to work. Her visits to his office had become more numerous, and the topics of her conversations had become a little more random. Landon could have instructed her to leave him alone so he could get some work done, but he didn't have the heart to say anything to her about her interruptions.

Instead, he chose to do something else. He just tuned her out so she would be less distracting. When she came into his office and chatted away, he didn't actually listen to what she said. He only pretended to listen. She would chatter for a while, and he would respond with those fatherly "Well that's good" or "Really?" or "Isn't that something" kinds of statements while he kept his mind on his work.

Kristin never caught on to what her dad was doing. The more she talked, the more she seemed to like the sound of her own voice. With her fairly constant verbiage, she gave her dad plenty of opportunities to practice his method of pseudo-communication. Their conversation developed a kind of cadence, with Kristin uttering words for a while and her dad giving his canned replies.

One morning, after Kristin and her dad carried on one of their so-called conversations, Landon found his wife, Emma, standing near his desk. She seemed to be concerned about something that had happened in one of his chats with Kristin. To make sure that Emma had Landon's undivided attention, she told him to shut down his computer, get out of his chair, and follow her.

Emma led Landon to the window overlooking the backyard and asked him to take a look. Through the window he could see Kristin. She appeared to be busy, working as if she was on an important mission. Then he noticed that she had her little arms full of her dolls. She took them to a beach towel that she had spread out on the grass. She gently laid each one of them on the beach towel with great care.

Surprised and a little befuddled by what he saw, Landon asked Emma, "What's Kristin doing? She's never taken her dolls into the backyard like that before."

"No, she hasn't." Emma replied. "That's why I wanted to show you what she was doing. Given the way you tune her out when she talks with you sometimes, I wondered if you realized what you promised her this morning."

"I made a promise to her?"

"Yes, you did. She asked you if you would build her a dollhouse, and you said, 'Yes, sweetheart.' She took you at your word and got busy taking her dolls outside so she can place them in the dollhouse once you've finished building it for her."

Landon knew what he had to do. First, he called his boss and said that he would be out of his office for a while. Then he went to the building supply store and bought some material to build a dollhouse. When he returned home, he got busy fulfilling the promise that he had made to Kristin. She believed him when he said that he would build her dollhouse. Landon intended to show her that he kept his promises.

In the Exodus and Philippians passages, adversity stands out as a major topic. Standing firm in adversity means relying on God to keep his promises. Unlike Landon, God is aware of his promises to his people. No one has to remind him.

Proper 21 / Pentecost 16 / Ordinary Time 26
Matthew 21:23-32
by John Smylie

Brokenness to Life

Back in the 1970s when I attended seminary in Cambridge, Massachusetts, there was an option to participate in a class about alcoholism. Alcoholism and addiction touched so many lives that the seminary felt it was important to offer a specific class at that time so we future ministers would be better able and more equipped to minister to the families we discovered in our congregations who suffer under this burden. My family was one of those ravaged by the disease of alcoholism. Back when I was three years old, my mother divorced my father for a number of reasons but the primary and perhaps the core reason was that he was an unrepentant and un-recovered alcoholic. He drank, he lied, he fooled around and was unfaithful, and eventually I learned he was even abusive. Now I wish this story had a happy ending, but it doesn't. He never stopped drinking, he never worked the AA twelve-step program, and the bottle remained his primary relationship.

As part of my healing process I wrote a song — songs are often touchstones that allow me to express deep feelings. The first verse of the song follows:

> He took a bottle for a bride.
> She promised him an easy ride.
> Does he know the lady lied,
> I pray someday he will.
>
> He's held for more than 30 years,
> Her hollow laughs her empty tears.

> And still he swallows all her fears,
> I pray he'll let her go.

I bring this up because while attending the seminary and taking the course as part of my own personal healing process, I had to attend a few AA meetings. First of all, to hear the stories of recovery and to discover the need for community among those who were gathered there was more powerful than the testimonies I've heard in most of the churches I've ever attended. Everyone there knew their need for a power greater than themselves to bring them to sanity. At the end of the meeting when the group gathered and prayed together the Lord's Prayer, it was if I was standing in front of a hurricane with 150-mile-an-hour wind blowing in my face. The prayer was intense, powerful, and more beautiful than I'd ever experienced in my life. These folks knew their need for God.

So I wonder as we look at the characters in the gospel and as we look at the characters at AA meetings and in our churches, with whom will God be more pleased. I think the temptation in church is to think that God needs us — while the clear message at AA is that we need God.

Now I'm not saying that folks in churches are bad and folks at AA meetings are good, but I am saying that we need to be careful with our Christianity. It seems that our Lord once again affirms a message that's not so obvious. He affirms the one who immediately says no but who changes his mind. He challenges the one who says yes, the one who looks good in the beginning, but doesn't follow through and get the work done.

When Johnny was in his teens, he had already fallen off the path his parents hoped that he would follow. He had experimented with alcohol, he had become friends with several different kinds of drugs, and he learned enough from watching pornography to overcome any natural fears that he might have about experimenting in sexual relations. In fact, he got a girl pregnant during his junior year in high school and after he learned of her pregnancy, he wanted nothing to do with her.

He wanted to live his life unencumbered. So he got on his motorcycle, didn't tell anyone where he was going, and left to live as a free spirit leaving his home to go across the country. He found folks along the way that would share in his drug habit and others to give him odd jobs to enable him to maintain his motorcycle and keep it full of gas. He quickly realized there weren't too many really good opportunities for him and as the days turned into months and months turned into a couple of years, he was haunted by the thought of the child and mother he left behind. Every now and then he'd have a dream — sometimes the dreams would come in the night — very often they came in the day as he attended to menial tasks. The glory of being a free-on-the-road guy was disappearing. He dreamt of the child — he dreamt of the girl he left behind — he dreamt of his family — he dreamt of the life he might've had, had he been more responsible.

One day he walked into a church and heard the preacher talk about the prodigal son and he knew the preacher was talking about him — calling him to go home. God had been clearly working on him through the dreams both night and day and through entering this church, he was at a place where he could hear this word as an invitation to life — a new life — a life that he'd left behind — a life that he could rediscover — a life filled with possibilities and hopes that had disappeared from view but now was back in sight more clearly than they'd ever been before.

He went home. He went to his old girlfriend and asked for her forgiveness and she said it would take her some time, but yes, he could come and see his child — their child. He asked his parents for forgiveness and like the prodigal son, they welcomed him home. By the grace of God, he put down his drugs and he picked up books and got his GED. Over time he reconciled with his girlfriend and became a pretty good dad offering child support, now hoping that one day the three of them could live together.

I've often wondered what it would have been like if he never left — if in his bitterness he'd married her in the beginning. Would he have been as tender as he is now — having learned the hard lessons of life that he learned on the road? Would he have been as compassionate had he never left home?

I think he's entered the kingdom of God having once visited the gates of hell. My hope for him is that in the days ahead, his deepest desire of being a family will be realized. Not every story has a happy ending, but one thing is sure: God is in every story and for that — for his presence — for his challenge — for his grace we give thanks.

Proper 22 / Pentecost 17 / Ordinary Time 27
Psalm 19
by Keith Hewitt

qGenesis

The room was dark. It smelled of alcohol, ozone, and just a hint of despair.

The source of the alcohol smell was easy to spot — a bottle of vodka stood on one corner of the desk, about a quarter empty; the tumbler next to it was completely empty. The ozone was a little harder to trace but casting about the room just a little pointed out the culprit soon enough — an array of servers, stacked on metal shelves, in one corner of the room, lights blinking silently as they pondered galaxies of 0s and 1s. That left the man behind the desk, staring at a widescreen monitor, as the source of despair.

"So there you are," his graduate assistant announced, after giving him a wasted moment or two to acknowledge her presence. "Are you okay, Doctor Kempthorne?"

"Here I am," he agreed, with barely a quiver in his voice to hint at where the quarter bottle of vodka had gone. "And, yes, I am o-flippin'-kay." He stared at the monitor as he spoke, never looking at his assistant.

"We missed you at the party," she said, studying the screen. At first, she thought it was turned off, but then she realized that the grayness on the screen had a form to it, a texture that flowed and changed subtly with the march of time. It was not the deliberate animation of a screensaver, but something more... and less. "The Chancellor wanted to introduce you to the Science Editor for the *Times*."

"I know. That's why I'm here."

"Really?" She picked up the vodka bottle, sloshed it around a little, then set it down and screwed on the cap. "I've never known you to be shy around the media, Doctor."

"Certainly not," he agreed. "I was the one who suggested the party in the first place to go with our news release. I was the one who told the Chancellor this would put the Advanced Computer Sciences Laboratory at the University of Wisconsin-Joliet on the media map. One story, one release, and for the next decade or two anyone who wanted to get an authoritative take on a story that had anything to do with quantum computing, or advanced evolutionary algorithmic simulation design, or even the next generation of flippin' videogames would come to us — the UWJ Advanced Computer Sciences Laboratory." He raised his head, 'til it almost flopped back on his neck and sniffed ostentatiously. "Do you smell it? That's grant money, my dear — the sweet, sweet smell of grant money flowing to our little corner of academia." He took a deep breath and let it out gustily. "Like blood to a vampire — the nourishment that keeps research scientists going."

She studied the man in the chair, trying to calculate what he might do next. Over two and a half years, she had seen him angry, she had seen him happy, she had seen him so lost in solving a particular problem that he would forget to eat, and would practically have to be coaxed to eat a sandwich. She had never seen him… this way. "So why are you here?" she asked, adding silently, *apart from the obvious*. Maybe it was stage fright?

"I am here," he said, with great deliberation, "exactly because of the research we're unveiling tonight, and all the hoopla that goes with it. I am here exactly because of all those earnest reporters down there in our auditorium, snarfing down snacks and press releases with equal relish."

"Are you afraid of crowds?" she guessed, giving voice to her silent thought.

He raised himself up to full sitting height and moved his feet crabwise so his chair would turn slowly to face his assistant. "I'll have you know I was an actor in college," he said with a flourish, giving a long "o" sound to actor. "I was in many productions, from Shakespeare to Ibsen, and I acted with such ferocity and depth that I was soon urged to go into a field where I would have less contact with human beings." He waved one finger back and forth, slowly, in admonishment. "The point is, I was never scared. I just wasn't very good."

His assistant smiled, in spite of herself, and asked, "Then why are you here, instead of in the auditorium, taking credit for your work and ingratiating yourself to the Science Editor of the *Times* and the producers of *Nova*?"

"I am here because of my work," he said simply.

"I don't understand," his assistant admitted after a moment. "What do you mean?"

"Consider why we are having the press conference," he said, his tone sliding from slightly stilted to something more professorial, more in the vein of a teacher instructing his class. "We are telling the world that we have developed the first practical, fully functioning quantum computer. A computer that is as far beyond the binary processing used in conventional computers as your laptop is ahead of the abacus. A single box that can do more calculations per second than all of those things put together —" he gestured toward the bank of servers in the corner. They squatted in the darkness, blinking back impassively.

She nodded. "Fully realized quantum computing is orders of magnitude more powerful than the fastest binary supercomputer," she quoted.

"Exactly. And with all that power at our fingertips, we developed a family of advanced evolutionary algorithmic simulation applications. With quantum data processing, we finally had a tool that could let us do the kinds of things we really wanted to do in the simulation arena. The advanced applications let us capture variables in quantities that were unthinkable before, and manipulate them in ways that were impossible a year ago."

He pushed himself up, toddled over to the rack of servers in the corner, regarded them sadly for a moment or two, one hand resting on the top of the rack. "Poor things," he murmured, stroking the warm metal with his hand, "they never saw it coming. Leading edge one day, and the next...." He turned away, dropped his hand to his side. "Did you ever see *Old Yeller*? It's time to take these things out to the corn crib and get it over with."

"One thing at a time," his assistant cautioned. "You still haven't told me why you're here. You — we — have succeeded beyond our wildest dreams."

"Hmm, yes — dreams. Indeed." He walked back around the desk, to his chair, talking as he walked — and taking great care, as the multitasking it required seemed to be almost beyond his reach. "You're familiar with the application, qGenesis?"

"It's one of the simulations, to study the origins of the universe and life."

"Yes. We worked with the physicists and the biologists and the chemists and the astronomers — everybody had a hand in that one. You feed in the originating parameters — say the conditions that existed at the time of the Big Bang — and overlay that with everything we think we know about physics, right down to the subatomic level. Then you throw the switch and watch what happens."

He dropped into the chair and took a deep breath. "The evolutionary algorithms will walk through every permutation of what might happen for any given circumstance, determine the probable outcome of every permutation, and then follow each path to its next logical step. And do it incredibly quickly." He pulled open a drawer in the desk, took out a piece of paper, began sketching on it. "Here, you have two clouds of dust and hydrogen floating in space, approaching each other. What happens?" From one point, he drew a line, "The clouds attract one another," he drew another line, "the clouds ignore one another," another line, "part of one cloud is attracted to the other," another line, "one of the clouds is composed of antimatter, and they annihilate one another."

"Then for each outcome, the application looks at what might happen next." He sketched branches from the end point of each line. "And so on, and so on — the quantum processing just keeps track of all of it, assigning probabilities to each outcome. You let it run billions of years, simulation-time, until we get to present-day. No matter, fifteen billion years of simulation-time will only take about ten or twelve days of iterations, our time."

He stopped sketching and tapped the paper with his pencil. "It's an incredibly powerful research tool. A physicist can look at all of the end-outcomes on qGenesis, and determine which one is closest to our actual universe. Once he chooses, all of the related events collapse into a single timeline, and he can trace it back. Step by step, he can watch stars form, he can see planets collect out of nothing — all the way back to the beginning. He can watch it all, understand which hypotheses worked, what events had to happen in what order, to get to what we have today."

His assistant nodded. "That was what we hoped for. A simulation so complete that it would not only tell you the outcome, but tell you why it happened."

"Exactly. And qGenesis can do the same thing with biology. We've theorized for decades about how the first amino acids became protogenes, and how they eventually evolved into life forms. qGenesis will be able to tell us that, too, once we have all of the parameters laid out. qGenesis will take us from organic molecules to that pinnacle of evolution, you — well, me. That's what I've been working on."

"And you suddenly realized that you weren't the pinnacle of evolution?"

"Oh, no, I am, all right. It's just that I had this sudden realization." He turned back to face the monitor, eyes lost in its shapeless dance. "I realized that for the application to get from Point A to Point B, we had to program what could happen at each step of the way. These two molecules can combine, these other two can't. Carbon can do this, this, and this, but not that." He lowered his voice. "And that's when I realized how well our little application simulates the real world — because without those rules in place, we wouldn't be here. Without the laws of physics, the universe never forms; without the laws of biochemistry, life never develops."

"Yess —" his assistant said uncertainly, drawing it out.

"So for all of this to be here," he said, sweeping an arm at the world around them, "For you and me to be here, the universe had to behave in a certain way." He looked at her, then. "You and I, the rest of our team — we wrote the rules for qGenesis. We did the programming. But somebody had to do the same for the universe. Somebody had to program it all. And until now, the thought had never crossed my mind — not as a real possibility."

"But randomness, chance, over billions of years can explain —"

"Randomness will only beget randomness," he answered. "I understand, now, that you can't get order from chaos unless there is a will to order, first."

"So you think —" she began, and trailed off.

"No," he said firmly, "I know." At that moment, a pinpoint of light appeared in the center of the formless gray on the monitor. It caught his attention, and he turned toward it. The pinpoint swelled, danced, and shimmered for a moment or two, and then exploded in a fury of white energy that flooded the screen.

"Let there be light," he said and wept softly in the glow.

Proper 23 / Pentecost 18 / Ordinary Time 28
Psalm 106:1-6, 19-23
by Craig Kelly

Second Chances

If he weren't in there dying already, I think I'd want to kill him.

I never asked him to get involved. He should have minded his own business. If he had just left well enough alone, everything would have turned out the way it was supposed to. I had it timed perfectly. There was no chance that it wouldn't work. But I didn't count on someone trying to play hero.

I saw that taxi coming from four blocks away. As fast as that guy was driving, I knew he wouldn't be turning anytime soon. At the speed he was driving, I knew it would do the job. I knew it would kill me.

All I had to do was walk into the street at just the right time so that he wouldn't have a chance to brake. Closer the yellow angel came, ready to end my pain, my suffering. I bolted off the sidewalk, on a direct collision course with my destiny. I blocked out the sounds of onlookers yelling at me, warning me to turn away from that which I most desired. They didn't understand. They couldn't.

As I stepped into the lane, looking at the two headlights at the end of my tunnel, I smiled. The car horn may as well have been an angelic chorus bidding me welcome. The crescendo was building as the screeching tires provided the accompaniment. It was all going to be over. I raised my hands, waiting for the final note.

I expected the lurch to come from in front of me as the bumper of the taxi knocked me off my feet, slamming my face into the hood or windshield. What I didn't expect was feeling a push from beside me, knocking me out of the taxi's trajectory. I heard the sound of a body hitting the taxi, being tossed onto the road. The ensuing screams confirmed my worst fears. Someone stole my deliverance!

Having failed in life, now I even failed in ending it! I was so ashamed, so humiliated! I never asked for help! Nobody ever cared before; why did someone have to care now? I just laid there in the street, weeping, wailing because not only do I have to continue my wretched existence, but now, because of me, there is more suffering in the world. Someone else is suffering because of me.

I said nothing as the paramedics examined me and my "rescuer." When the police and counselors questioned me, I told them the truth: Life was unbearable for me and I just wanted it over. I never wanted anyone else to get hurt. By some miracle, they didn't press charges, but now I'm here in the hospital, antidepressants coursing through my veins. Here I am, standing in front of the door of my rescuer's room, seeing him bruised and beaten, a ventilator helping him breathe, delaying his inevitable journey, the one I was supposed to make. I see the man's wife sitting beside his bed, holding his hand, wiping tears from her face with the other. She sees me; I should go.

"Hey!" she calls. I want to run, but for some reason, I stop. She comes out of the room, looking at me. "You're the guy my husband saved, aren't you?"

I'm not sure what to say, but her eyes look for an answer. "Yes," I finally get out. I wait for the screams, the fists beating against my chest as she laments the fact that it's her husband dying and not me. I know I deserve it. Yet, as the moments pass, she just stands there, looking at me. Sniffing, she looks at me, and I can see in her eyes that there is no hatred, just empathy. "Are you all right?"

What? How can she ask me that? I killed her husband! I may as well have pointed a gun at him and shot him dead!

I'm the reason she's here crying in a hospital rather than at home living her comfortable life. And she wants to know if I'm all right?

"I think so," I mumble. "They gave me some medication, and they say I should be okay." I'm trying so hard to keep my composure, but I can feel the tears forming, pooling, finally slipping down my face. "Lady, I'm so sorry. I never meant for anyone to get hurt. I just...."

She doesn't say anything, just rushes to me and embraces me. Wait... what? She's actually holding me! Why? I've hurt her; I've inflicted a pain on her that will be with her for life; why does she embrace me? Why is she telling me it's going to be okay?

"Why? Why are you doing this?" I manage to get out between sobs.

Her tears mingle with mine as she holds me close. "I know you didn't want to hurt anyone. I know you must be hurting so much to want to end it all like that. It will be okay. It will be okay." She just keeps repeating it, soothing me as a mother soothes her newborn child.

"Why did he do it? I was nobody to him. Why did he have to save me?"

She steps away from me, looking into my eyes. "You were in trouble. He had to help. That was just how my husband was. Nobody was a nobody to him, and nobody's a nobody to me." She smiles. Even after all this, she smiles at me. I don't think I'll ever understand this. I just stare at her, trying to understand why she can be so kind and so loving after everything I've done to her. Finally, after standing in silence in the hall for who knows how long, she speaks. "I need to get back to my husband. Could you do me a favor?"

"Sure, anything." In amazement, I realize that I actually mean it. I would even trade places with her husband if I could, not to die and end my pain, but to die and end hers.

"Honor my husband."

"How?" I desperately want to fulfill her wish, but I don't even understand what she wants. Does she think I'm a sculptor and can build him a statue? Or a great orator who will bring the world to tears telling them of his selflessness and sacrifice? What does she want me to do?

She squeezes my shoulder. "Live. Live a life worthy of what my husband gave up for you. I can think of no greater tribute to him."

I just stare at her. What do I say? Can I go back to the mess I wanted so desperately to leave behind? I want to leave, to give her the litany of reasons why I can't go back to my life. Yet, there her husband is, unlikely to ever see another sunrise, and here I am, with a chance to start over. "I will," I finally tell her. "I promise you I will."

There's her smile again. "Thank you. Thank you so much. Take care of yourself, and God bless you." After hugging me one more time, she walks slowly back to her dying husband, leaving me stunned in the hallway.

I'm not sure how long I've been standing here, but I'm suddenly brought back to reality by the touch of a hand on my shoulder. I turn quickly to see a nurse standing beside me.

"Are you okay, honey?"

I don't know why, but I start to smile. "I... um... I think I'm going to be."

The nurse smiles back. "Good. Why don't we get you back to your room?"

As we start to walk together, I ask her, "Hey, before we get back to the room, do you think you could show me where the chapel is?"

She's still smiling. "Sure. Be glad to." She takes my hand as we walk to the elevator.

Proper 24 / Pentecost 19 / Ordinary Time 29
Matthew 22:15-22
by Scott Dalgarno

We Are, None of Us, Our Own

Jesus could smell a trap. When men linked to those he knew were hostile to him asked him to take an explicit and dangerous stand on whether Jews should or should not pay taxes to the Roman occupation of Judea he was clearly on his guard. The Pharisees anticipated that Jesus would oppose the tax, for Luke's gospel explains their purpose was "to hand him over to the power and authority of the governor." The governor was Pilate, and he was, of course, the man responsible for collecting Rome's taxes in Judea.

Jesus first called them hypocrites, and then asked one of them to produce a Roman coin, asking further that they identify the image on it. When they did he said, simply, "Render unto Caesar what is Caesar's, and unto God what it God's."

Anyone who thinks this is a straightforward answer in favor of the separation of church and state need think again. One need only note that Matthew tells us when the disciples of the Pharisees heard this "they were amazed." More is going on here than Jesus simply reassuring them that Caesar was an independent secular authority that God deemed autonomous. A lot more.

I mean, look, what belongs to Caesar that does not belong to God, anyway? Name me one thing… I'm waiting…. Maybe it was only the image on the coin Jesus asked them to supply for the lesson.

When it comes to dealing with the authorities of his day, Jesus was a sly one. Remember that it was he, himself, who told his disciples, "See, I am sending you out like sheep among wolves. So be as cunning as serpents and as innocent as doves."

Jesus clearly "amazed" them because he could give them an answer without having to step in their carefully laid trap; without having to pay for it with his life. Besides, it's one of those questions everyone should spend his or her life answering for themselves; discovering for themselves how true it is that everything — our houses, our forests, our spouses, our children, our very lives, belong 100% to God.

For my money (ha) the story isn't about Caesar at all — it's about us and it's about God.

Here's a true story with a connection to "Caesar" that illustrates some of what I mean. I have changed the names.

* * *

It was 1965 and Lisa had just gotten out of the state mental hospital. She wasn't crazy, exactly; her life had just been impossible. She was 19, with no home, no husband, no money, no place to go, and she just had a baby.

The state had already "stated" that she would be giving the baby up for adoption. She would need to sign the papers, of course, but the social worker in charge of her case acted as if she had no other choice. A foster home was waiting for the baby.

But Lisa had read a news story about foster homes recently and many of them were under investigation — many foster parents were caring but too many had been identified as dumping grounds where children were being "placed" for money alone. Lisa knew what it was like to grow up unloved. She knew this too well.

When a nurse spotted her breast-feeding her baby in the maternity ward she asked Lisa why she was bothering, since welfare was coming for the baby in three days time. Lisa explained that she had read about colostrums — how the first three days of breast feeding gives the baby the kind of immunity that can pay dividends the child's whole life long.

The nurse, who had hardly looked at Lisa now looked deeply into her young eyes. Moments later she was instructing Lisa on how to better hold the baby during the feeding to ensure the best digestion.

"We need to get you some clothes for her," she said. "Clothes?" said Lisa. "I thought the foster family would provide those."

"There isn't going to be a foster family," said the nurse. "You're going to keep her. God put her into your care, not the care of anyone else."

"But I don't even know how to diaper a baby," she said.

"You're going to learn right now," she said, and with that she led Lisa to a room full of dolls, cotton diapers, and pins. The lesson took ten minutes. Then she led Lisa back to the ward and announced to the other new mothers, "Miss W. is keeping her baby. Can each of you donate a piece of clothing from your layettes?"

One mother held up a nightshirt, another a receiving blanket, a third gave her a blue fleece bunting. The nurse showed up with a stack of diapers complete with pins.

Before welfare showed up, Lisa found herself in a home for mothers like herself where she was given even more.

That baby grew up into a fine woman and has given Lisa three grandchildren now; that and the knowledge it takes being a parent to learn that our children are charges put into our trust. Not possessions, but a means to learn the most important lesson of living, that we, none of us, are Caesar's, or even our own.

Proper 25 / Pentecost 20 / Ordinary Time 30
Matthew 22:34-46
by Argile Smith

Who's the Real Boss?

Ned's business seemed to be in serious trouble. He owned a small trucking company that showed great promise when he opened his doors for business ten years earlier. Back then, he couldn't keep up with the orders that came his way. He expanded a little sooner than he intended, but at the time he really didn't think that he had a choice. As he told himself and his employees at the time, he had to make hay while the sun was shining.

Those were the good old days for him and his trucking company. Now things were different. The number of orders had dropped to a frighteningly low level, and the cost of diesel fuel had gone through the ceiling. Some of his equipment needed serious attention. He could see costly maintenance bills peeking at him from around the corner, not to mention the bill he would receive for some necessary upgrades in some of his equipment.

Seeing that the company was in trouble, a number of his employees had moved on to other opportunities. In a way, Ned breathed a sigh of relief when his operation began to downsize by attrition, and he wondered about how long he could hold on to the remainder of his employees.

Although he hated to give up any of them, he had grown particularly fond of Brandon, a young man who worked part time for him. Brandon was a student at the local community college, and he approached Ned about working for his company while he studied business at college. Ned appreciated Brandon's willingness to work for not much more than minimum wage, and he admired the young man's eagerness to learn how to build a business "from the ground up."

The tough times forced Ned to make a decision about whether or not he could keep Brandon on the payroll. After determining that Brandon could learn from the experience of watching a business go belly-up, he decided not to dismiss him. Instead, he decided to talk to Brandon and tell him about the trouble the business had been facing and the poor prospects for keeping the doors open.

As he talked with Brandon, he commented on the building his company had leased. He explained that the landlord had been gracious in the past, always giving him a little more time to make his lease payments. Now he wondered if he ought to ask his landlord for a heavy dose of grace again in view of the fact that a little more time may not help the company's position.

Brandon listened to Ned, and after a while, he replied, "Ned, if you would like, I will be happy to talk to the landlord for you."

Ned chuckled and said, "Young man, you are kind, but I doubt that you should be placed in such a position. After all, you're a young man working part-time for me. With all due respect to your eagerness to help, the landlord wouldn't take you seriously."

"Oh, yes, she would." Brandon said confidently. "She's my aunt, and she's the person who told me to work with you so you could teach me how to build a business from the ground up." Brandon went on to say that some time ago she had decided to entrust her rather substantial business holdings to him. She wanted him to take her business interests and grow them. That's why she wanted him to get some practical business experience.

"My aunt appreciates you for what you are doing to help me. I am certain that she will work with you to help you through this tough time."

Surprised by what Brandon had just told him, Ned realized that the young man who referred to him as a boss actually had a great deal of authority over him. In the same way, the sovereign Lord to whom Moses prayed supervised his work from eternity (Psalm 90), and the Lord who was the son of David also supervised David's work from eternity as well (Matthew 22:34-46).

Reformation Day
John 8:31-36
by Craig Kelly

Free Indeed

> *So Jesus said to the Jews who had believed in him, "If you abide in my word, you are truly my disciples, and you will know the truth, and the truth will set you free... So if the Son sets you free, you will be free indeed."*
>
> — John 8:31-32, 36

He stood silent, trying to stay perfectly still while continually fighting the urge to shiver uncontrollably. True, the tiny, stone-walled room was filled with cold, damp, musty air, but that was only part of what gave his muscles the almost irresistible urge to spasm. Sweat poured down his face, the salty liquid stinging the open cuts on his forehead and cheek, dripping over the mottled skin that had swollen his left eye shut. His shoulders burned as his wrists were chained above his head to the cold, clammy stones. He reeked of sweat, stale urine, and fear.

* * *

Her shoulders protested bitterly at being held in such an unnatural position. However, with her wrists tied together behind her back, there was little she could do to offer her shoulders any relief. Her bare feet also ached, the pain migrating up her legs. Being forced to stand in place continually for days would do that. She thanked God when her extremities numbed.

* * *

His lips moved rapidly, yet soundless, as he mumbled ancient prayers that bubbled up in his memory, anything he could think of to call for divine deliverance. But none had yet come, and he had been standing there for… for… four days? Five? Maybe a week. He wasn't sure. One minute, one hour seemed to blend into the next, distorting any perception of passing time. The only breaks in his intolerable solitude was when a guard would come in and either beat him or stuff a hard crust of bread in his mouth, cutting the inside of his cheek. When the guard dumped a cup of water in his mouth, he almost choked to death.

* * *

She was taken two weeks ago, dragged from her bed in the middle of the night. As the wife of an underground pastor, it was thought that seeing her suffer would force her husband to give the police the names of other leaders in the illegal church. As much as she suffered, she thanked God every day she remained in captivity, knowing that her imprisonment meant that her brothers and sisters in the faith were safe. The horrors she was forced to endure were a small price to pay for the advancement of the gospel.

* * *

More time passed. Just him, the cold, and his prayers. Finally the bolted door opened, letting in a piercing light that made him recoil, a reflexive reaction that sent fire through his stiff muscles. His knees buckled, allowing his body to tumble helplessly toward the frigid stone floor, stretching his already stressed shoulder, pulling it out of joint. He let out a cry, but in his weakened condition, it was more of a whimper. The guard, clad in his tarnished armor, laughed at this pathetic display. He slowly walked up to the prisoner, stooping down one on knee to look at him directly, their faces only inches apart.

" 'Aving a good morning, are we?" he sneered, his breath reeking of ale. "I hope so, because when the inquisitor gets 'ere, your day will get a lot worse. Of course, if you are ready to recant and put this foolishness be'ind you, I'm sure things would look much better for you." He snickered again, inching his face even closer. As if relaying a closely guarded secret, the guard whispered, "Between you and me, I 'ope you don't. More fun for me."

The prisoner tried to hold back the tears. He knew what the guard meant, and he knew what he was in for if he didn't recant. Every cell in his body seemed to scream at him, begging him to do whatever it took to avoid that torture. The phrase, "I will recant" even seemed to begin to make its way up his throat, just waiting for his mouth to open.

* * *

The guard left smirking, chuckling as he finished another "session" with his prisoner. After having his way with her, he, in his "mercy," left her huddled in a corner of the cell, rather than forcing her to stand. He must have been in a good mood; he even untied her hands before he left. Pity, perhaps? After everything he had done to her, it was hard to imagine him as the sympathetic type.

As the cell door slammed, the lock latching into place, she wept, desperately trying to keep silent so as to not give the guard another excuse to come in. "God, how much more of this can I take?" she whispered through her tears. "I'm trying so hard, but I don't think I can take this. I can't do it, Lord, I can't!" She leaned her head back against the stone wall, overwhelmed by grief and fear.

* * *

"Do you recant of your heresy?" the inquisitor asked. Clothed in fine purple and scarlet linens, he seemed grossly out of place in this dark dungeon colored in shades of black and gray. "Do you agree to acknowledge your sin publicly, putting aside these foolish notions of 'grace alone' and that the Bible is the only source of revelation for Christians? Put aside your folly, and come back to the church, and we will embrace you."

Barely able to move after the torture he was forced to endure, he slowly raised his head to speak.

* * *

As she sat in the corner of her cell, the tears finally slowing, she noticed a small gap between the stone bricks along the wall, and it appeared as though there was something stuffed inside. Desperate to think of anything other than the horrors she endured, she leaned over and peered in the hole, seeing what appeared to be a piece of paper that had been crumpled and forced into it. Using her little finger, the only one that could fit in the gap, she managed to work the paper out, watching it drop on the floor. Quickly she darted her eyes to the door to see if she aroused any attention. Finally confident that she was undetected, she picked up the paper and smoothed it out. It was a strip of paper from a Bible translated into her native language. It must have been left by whoever previously occupied that cell. She began to read:

* * *

"If you abide in my word, you truly are my disciples...."

* * *

"And you will know the truth...."

* * *

"And the truth shall set you...."

* * *

"Free...."

* * *

"...So if the Son sets you free...."

* * *

"You will be free indeed."

* * *

The prisoner met the inquisitor's disbelieving gaze, meeting it not with anger, fear, or panic, but with a calm resolve, even going so far as to feel love and empathy for his captors. He knew what his statement meant. He knew what would become of him. Yet he knew he could not be silent. He would not be silent.

"My lord, I know I am in chains, and I know that this answer will mean my death. But my heart is not chained. My spirit is not captive. I am already free. Whether I live or die, if I walk out of this cell to be released or to be burned, I am free. Praise God, I'm free."

* * *

Slowly, the tortured wife began to smile. Even though every muscle in her face ached, the smile did not dim. Instead, it grew until it was joined by a quiet giggle. She leaned her head back against the wall, no longer overwhelmed by fear, but now overcome by joy. Despite the pain, she began to clap her bruised, bloody hands together and, tears rolling down her cheeks, she began to sing.

All Saints Day
Revelation 7:9-17
by John Smylie

The Fifth Gospel

If you ever have an opportunity to visit the Holy Land, you will probably discover the Jerusalem cross. The Jerusalem cross consists of five crosses; there is one large cross in the center and on each of the four corners there are four small crosses. Some interpret the meaning of the five crosses as representing the four corners of the world — east, west, north, and south with Jerusalem and the Holy Land in the center, symbolizing the entire world coming to Christ. An interpretation that I like to place on the Jerusalem cross is this: The four crosses represent the four gospels, Matthew, Mark, Luke, and John. The cross in the center represents the land — the Holy Land — the fifth gospel.

The Holy Land is a land of contrasts. To the east, it is bordered by the Mediterranean Sea. To the north, it is bordered by Lebanon and Syria. The western border includes Syria and Jordan and to the south, we find Egypt. The northern part of the country is more fertile as there are three primary sources of water that feed the Jordan River that then flows into the Sea of Galilee and out of the Sea of Galilee ending in the Dead Sea. South of the Dead Sea and around the Dead Sea, the land is extremely barren. It's what we know as the Judean wilderness, and wilderness it is. Water is perhaps the most precious commodity in all of the Holy Land. Wars continue to be fought over water — negotiations often center around water — and in the imagery of Revelation where we discover the lamb at the center of the throne will be their shepherd, and he will guide them to springs of the water of life because this is exactly what the people of the land need and long for.

At times, it may be difficult for us in this country to recognize the value of water. Most of us have indoor plumbing connected to city reservoirs or wells. We turn on the tap and out flows your drinkable water. We step into the shower and are bathed in the sweet and relaxing flow and blessing of hot streams pulsing upon our bodies. Some of us may be blessed with large bathtubs with jets in the sides of them that circulate the water massaging our bodies. Others may be blessed with swimming pools and hot tubs and a few may even have water coolers where fresh, clean, and purified water is delivered directly on an as needed basis. The luxury that we have with water was virtually unknown to the people of the Bible except for kings like King Herod with his thousands of slaves. We are extremely blessed and our blessings may have made us dull to the blessings of water and to the abundance of the life that we now enjoy in this country even in the midst of financial crises, rising inflation, lowering housing values, and all the other transitory challenges that come our way — we remain a very blessed people.

There was a certain professor whose class on the New Testament I took at Gordon Conwell Theological Seminary just north of Boston. (Gordon Conwell was a part of the Boston Theological Institute a consortium of schools, which provided an opportunity for students from each seminary to be cross fertilized and exposed to other traditions.) Gordon Conwell was a more evangelical seminary than the seminary that I attended and I desired to be exposed to the evangelical teaching and biblical perspective that was taught in that place. But when it came to the book of Revelation the professor had come to the conclusion that the whole book ought to be viewed as a kind of motion picture. He advised the class not to read it literally but to allow the images that make up the book of Revelation to work upon our consciousness.

He was not interested in breaking it down with a view toward figuring it out in a way that it described and predicted the future. Rather he invited the students in his class to be washed by the images and to allow the images to impact us, to go with them, and discover where they would lead us. As I consider his teaching method for the book of Revelation, my conclusion is this — he didn't understand it and rather than trying to explain something that was beyond his comprehension he was inviting us to simply receive the word while opening ourselves to it.

Over the years, I've had four opportunities to spend time in the Holy Land. My first visit was in 1976 — my last visit was in September of 2008. Perhaps it's because I'm getting older but it seems to me each visit becomes a bit more distressing than the last.

On three of the four visits including the one just a few weeks ago I had the opportunity to view the plains of Armageddon. The plains of Armageddon are part of a trade route connecting north and south as well as a route to connect the east and west. On the plains of Armageddon, battle after battle has been fought to control the commerce that passed through the land. When one visits the place, one visits a hill upon which ruins have been discovered that date back thousands of years. Strongholds were built so that the trade routes could be fortified, but in those days when battles were fought, one of the ways that communities would be overcome was through cutting them off from their well — their source of water. In this community, which is now operated by a kibbutz, there is a tunnel from the city dug to the well. The well was outside of the city but there was a way of covering up the outer entrance to the well to make it invisible to whatever soldiers were coming at that time. There are 183 steps leading down to the well and to the tunnel, which itself is quite long and cut out of stone. Generally, it was the women who would carry the jugs of water down the stairs and through the tunnel filling their jugs and then carrying them back to their homes, not only to care for their families, but also to water the animals. They would tie lanterns to their feet because their hands were consumed with holding the water jars above their heads. Here is another example of why water was so valuable, imagine what a blessing it would be to the women to understand, to hear, and to hope that the lamb at the center of the throne will be their shepherd and that he would guide them to springs of water and life — springs that would not be down 183 stairs and through a dark tunnel. Imagine the joy they felt at the vision and hope that the lamb at the center of the throne who will be their shepherd who will not only guide them to the springs of water of life but to God who will wipe away every tear from their eyes. There would be no more tears brought upon all the people because of the hardship of their lives — no more tears brought to them because of the constant battles with their enemies and the death of loved ones. Tears at seeing their labors destroyed would be gone, as would the tears shed because they lacked the necessary sustenance needed to keep their children alive.

There remains great suffering in the land of Israel. There is so much fear still present in the land — fear of the enemies that are on the borders. The Jews fear the Palestinians and the Palestinians remain in an occupied country in their own land. Israel today is one land, two nations, and three religions.

The words of Revelation that we read today are words of hope for the people of old, and they can be words of hope to us as well. Yet when I consider the hardship that I face compared to the hardship that was faced in the generations before me, I must confess that I live in a nation and in a time of abundance and in many ways the vision of the kingdom is already present right here in today — in this moment — in my life. So I suppose my challenge is to find and be open to ways where God's grace, which is so present in my life, can be channeled through me to others. Please join me in blessing others as we seek to wear within our souls and hearts, minds and spirit, a life of thanksgiving for the abundance that is ours — not only physical abundance but a spiritual abundance because we know the lamb who is at the center of the throne — the lamb who is the good shepherd, Jesus Christ.

Proper 26 / Pentecost 21 / Ordinary Time 31
Psalm 107:1-7, 33-37
by Frank Ramirez

A Magical Little Poem

Then they cried to the Lord in their trouble, and he delivered them from their distress....
— Psalm 107:6

My grandmother, my father's mother, was born Maria Galvan. She was born in Mexico. But in 1910, when she was ten years old, she moved with her family to the little town of Fierro in New Mexico, high in the mountains. Her father, Jesus Malgosa de Galvan, had heard of the thriving Hanover Mining Company and figured the people there would need a little store.

Her life was so different than mine. She was thirteen years old when she married Antonio Ramirez in 1913, and she went on to have thirteen children. Unfortunately, infant mortality was high in that region, and only seven survived to adulthood. Her husband died young, so for the last forty years of her life she wore black.

Grandma Mary did not speak much English and toward the end of her life she chose not to speak any at all. However, when I was a child we'd struggle to communicate. My Spanish wasn't very good and her English, though better, was halting. During my childhood, she'd come over to help when my mother was off having a baby, which in those days was all the time. I'm the second oldest of eight.

Though we had trouble communicating, she taught us by example. Grandma Mary was a great reader, for instance. She'd had very little formal schooling, but she read voraciously. We observed that and were great readers ourselves.

(When she died, I was given her copy of *Don Quixote* — in Spanish, of course.)

The greatest lesson she gave us was when we'd incur one of those inevitable childhood injuries, like a scraped knee or elbow. When we ran indoors crying she'd give us a "sana, sana."

Grandma would lean over the cut or scrape, wave her hand over the wound, and recite:

> *Sana, sana,*
> *Colita de rana.*
> *Si no sanas hoy*
> *Sanarás Mañana.*

And that was usually good enough. We'd take off running for more play — and more scrapes. Sana, sana.

I've learned over the years that the poem wasn't just something Grandma knew. It's known over the whole Hispanic world. Folks from other countries brighten when I recite the poem. Their grandmothers used it too. You can find it in children's books, on posters, and postcards.

But what did the poem mean?

It meant something like "wellness, wellness, gas from a frog. If you don't get well today, you'll get well tomorrow."

The second line was pure nonsense, but the rest of it made sense! If you don't get well today, you'll get well tomorrow.

Maybe that poem didn't actually cure us, but it healed us. Our little scrapes were still wide open. The most we might get was a bandage. But that didn't matter. We were healed. Most dings are not as bad as we first think.

That poem brought the magic gift of perspective. Just wait. It will get better. Most everything does.

That's one gift we can give to each other in times of distress — the gift of perspective. We know what's important and what can wait. We know that, like a car, when we first hear a rattle or a thump, you just ignore it. It'll either go away or it'll get worse, and then you'll know what to do about it.

Perspective. This is not the end of the world. Those of us who are a little older have seen the end of the world. We've stood at the edge of the abyss and looked over the edge. We've seen. And life goes on.

Perspective teaches us that life is short. Eat dessert first. It's why we know how important it is to embrace joy right now.

The psalmist celebrates that when the people called aloud in their distress, God provided deliverance! Sometimes we think that deliverance means removal of our problems, curing our sicknesses, restoring everything the way it was. Sometimes healing, deliverance, renewal means learning to live with our cross for today and to triumph! It helps if we've been through this sort of thing before, because we know God delivers!

Proper 27 / Pentecost 22 / Ordinary Time 32
Joshua 24:1-3a, 14-25
by Craig Kelly

As for Me and My House...

I've always been told that if you train a child in the way he should go, when he's old he won't be departed... or something like that. Basically, it means if you do right by your kids, they'll do right when they get older. I know it's in the Bible, but I can't begin to tell you where right now.

Well, there were times when I believed that. I just figured if I could raise my two kids with the right values and the right direction, they would turn out all right. Of course, being a widower working at the local GM factory didn't exactly make things easy, what with having to drop kids off at babysitters or leaving notes for them to read after school letting them know there were TV dinners in the freezer for them when I worked second shift, but somehow, we seemed to make it through. Even took them to church every week, getting the good book into them, making sure they knew about God and his love and what the Bible says is right and wrong. My daughter even sang in the church choir for most of her teen years. Most beautiful soprano voice I've ever heard.

My son was an altar boy — even got to read the scriptures every now and then. He was good at speaking in public like that. I always thought that between that and his skills on the basketball court, he'd end up in the NBA and then doing TV commentary when he got older. He always said he wanted to play for the Bulls... be just like Michael Jordan. If things had gone differently, maybe he would have.

Seems like those days were a couple of lifetimes ago, now. Now, I'm here, sitting in a waiting area at the county jail, waiting to pick up my son. Amazing what getting in the wrong crowd will do to you. It started innocently enough. My son needed a new basketball to practice at home with. I couldn't get one — plant was on shutdown and money was tight — so some punk kid at school bought him one — plus new basketball shoes. Once he gained my son's confidence and friendship, it didn't take long to see where this kid was getting his money. Once he got my son into doing some dealing for him, it just went all downhill. Drug dealing, drinking, fights with other dealers, finally leading to that terrible day.

Can you imagine how torn you would feel, watching your son being wrestled to the ground in your own home by police officers? It's your son, your flesh and blood, and everything in you wants to jump in there and fight off his attackers, and yet you know that what they're doing to him is right. For the good of society, they need to pull his arms behind his back, handcuff him, and lead him away. I never felt so helpless in all my life.

I remember as they lifted him up off the ground, he began screaming and cursing at them, kicking up his legs vainly trying to get away. At one point, he lost his balance, slamming his shoulder against the kitchen wall. The force of the impact sent a decorative plate down to the ground, breaking it in three pieces. Things were so crazy, I didn't even notice it till my daughter and I got back from the station. It was given to my wife and I by her mother on our wedding day, inscribed with my wife's favorite scripture: "As for me and my house, we will serve the Lord." Seemed oddly appropriate that it was now broken, given the circumstances. I remember picking up what was left of the plate and slowly walking to the trash bin. I just figured it was time to clean up and move on.

"Dad! What are you doing? You told us that was Mom's favorite plate!"

It seemed like my daughter was instantly beside me, her hand on my shoulder.

"Look, it's time to clean up. No sense keeping a broken plate."

"What are you talking about? Just because it's broken doesn't mean you throw it away. If we work at it, it can be fixed." I still wonder if she was really talking about the plate. She worked well into the night, carefully applying the crazy glue, gently working the pieces back into place. The next morning, I walked into the kitchen to find the plate back upon the wall, back in one piece. The only way you would know it was broken is the three fine lines that run through the plate, but you have to be looking closely to find them. As I wait here for my son to be released, I wonder if our own family can come back together as easily.

My thoughts are interrupted by the sound of an opening door at the end of the room. My daughter and I stand together nervously, waiting to see who comes through. I don't know whether or not the man who comes through the door will be the same boy I raised... or if he'll be someone else.

Slowly, my son walks through the door, head down. He doesn't look like he's aged a day, and yet he looks older at the same time. As he lifts his head and spots us, I can see tears pooling in his eyes and I feel those same tears forming in my own. Suddenly he breaks out into a run, collapsing into me, sobbing. I join him. Never thought I'd sob in the open like this, but somehow it doesn't seem to matter right now. The three of us join in a tearful hug. It's over now. Finally over.

"Dad, I'm so sorry. I'm so sorry. I'm ready to change, Dad, I'm ready," he sobs into my chest.

"It's all right, son, it's all right. Come on, let's all go home."

Slowly, we walk out of the room, arm in arm.

Proper 28 / Pentecost 23 / Ordinary Time 33
Matthew 25:14-30
by C. David McKirachan

Monster Dandruff

My journey through life has offered opportunities at every turn. When I was unemployed after seminary I had opportunities to pump gas and work in a leather factory. I learned things and grew in ways that I am very grateful for. One would think the ministry would be such a place, full of fertile ground in which to grow and become and develop. But the ministry is a job. It entails a lot of meeting deadlines, going through the motions, living up and down to expectations — just like any other job.

One of the hardest disciplines for me is to deal with the day to day, the routine, and not get buried under the monster dandruff. When I was green in the business, I made sure that I adopted mentors. I visited them regularly and pumped them for hows, whens, wheres, and brilliant tidbits that I could claim and use to make things work. One of these saints shared with me that the people would put up with just about anything I had to say as long as I "paid the rent." I asked him what that entailed. Very simply, visit them — or more accurately, let it be known that you are visiting them. He told me most of them don't want you to come to their house, but they want to know that you are doing that for the people that "really need it." I thought that was rather cynical. After thinking about it I realized that what they need to know is that we care about them on a personal level. That's how they figure it out. Okay, it made sense. But putting it into action, getting out of the church — away from classes to teach, counseling sessions, and crises to deal with — was hard. Breaking the inertia of my priorities to sit with someone who didn't really have any pressing problems seemed... like paying rent. The drifts of bits and pieces of hours and days, of routine business, of times when inspiration seemed far away and a cup of coffee was my only defense against fatigue, all of it piled up and made it hard to let light shine.

Back in the days when I played and sang in bars and coffeehouses and anyplace I could get a gig, I learned a trick. Most of the time people don't listen to you. They treat you like elevator music and ignore your efforts to bring beauty and soul into the moment. So I used to sing to one or two people in the room who seemed to be paying attention. And if it was a hard house where no one was with me, I'd try to worm into the song and let it speak through me. I'd put me into the song.

So I started to do that with my visits. I'd try to find something about the person to celebrate. If they were ornery or nasty, I'd wrap the moment around me and try to find something interesting or hopeful in the environment. It started out as a survival mechanism, evolved to a habit, and now I treasure it as a gift.

It's easy to get buried. There is so much that sandbags our gifts and makes our moments dim and difficult. But we are gifted. We are gifts, if we are willing to invest ourselves in the moment.

But honestly, sometimes it ain't easy.

Christ the King (Proper 29) / Ordinary Time 34
Ezekiel 34:11-16, 20-24
by Craig Kelly

Diamonds

> *For thus says the Lord God: Behold, I, I myself will search for my sheep and will seek them out... I will seek the lost, and I will bring back the strayed, and I will bind up the injured, and I will strengthen the weak....*
>
> — Ezekiel 34:11, 16

A diamond in the rough... finding something precious in an unexpected or unattractive place. I've heard the phrase used so many times in movies or news articles that the diamond is starting to lose some of its luster. "Wow, the former moving company driver now plays right tackle for the Lions... sure found a real diamond in the rough there!" "I can't believe they found that rapper living out of his car out in the projects... looks like they found a real diamond in the..." — you get the idea. The phrase usually finds its way into some rags-to-riches story, something to make you feel good, like there's a chance you too can defy the odds and claw your way to greatness. Kind of ties in with the whole American Dream thing, doesn't it?

Sad part is, it's so easy nowadays to just see the rough. It's becoming harder to dig in the dirt and unearth the diamonds, so many people don't really feel like trying anymore. Just ask me. I was like that.

I live in a small city, a small, poor city. The area I live in kind of accentuates the poor part. When you drive by and see old men sitting listlessly on the porch of an abandoned house, their stubbly faces drawn, their eyes blank, staring off at nothing, or when you see young men looking around nervously, quickly ducking into a back alley to complete a drug deal, or when you see young women in tight dresses walking along the sidewalk, hoping to sell their souls every night to make a few bucks... yeah, diamonds can seem pretty rare among all the rough. Probably why they're so valuable.

I moved here from out of the area. I had no idea what I was getting myself into. Naïve doesn't even begin to describe my state of mind when I came here. Is ultra-naïve a word? Not that I was raised badly or anything like that. It was just that this kind of life was so far removed from where I came from. I used to live on a farm in the middle of the country. City life wasn't exactly second nature to me.

And yet here I am, here at home in the city. And here I am, helping with a Sunday school mission to kids here in the neighborhood. Every Sunday, I find myself in a small room helping to dish out a hot meal to 20-30 kids ranging from 5 to 15, cleaning up after them, and then helping to teach them about God, the Bible, and how to live the Christian life. I'm telling you, I never even thought I'd ever work with kids, let alone kids from a poor neighborhood! Now, I'm not going to claim credit for this ministry, like it was my vision or anything. Two ladies in my church had already started it and they came to a group of us for help once more kids started coming in. My wife and I were two of the people that were recruited to help out. I think when I started, I was basically crowd control. You know, make sure the kids don't get too out of hand, help out here and there if a kid had a question, stuff like that. I was just glad to help out.

I guess I didn't realize how much this ministry would impact my life.

I'll admit, when I started there was a part of me that would look at these kids coming in, some of them with dirty, worn-out clothes, some of them with chips on their shoulders the size of Lake Erie, and would think, "Why can't they just clean up a little bit? We have a Wal-Mart; can't they buy a decent shirt? Just for once, can we have that one come in here without the attitude?" Yet, over time, I have come to see that appearances don't necessarily tell the whole story. Maybe the mother got laid off and has to focus on buying food rather than new shirts for her kids. Maybe that kid is angry at the world because he only has anger waiting for him at home every night.

And maybe, just maybe, God loves these kids anyway, just the way they are.

Maybe, just maybe, he wants them to know him, whether they live in a stable, prosperous home or not.

Maybe he's willing to seek them out, wherever they come from, whatever their background, because he loves them that much.

Maybe he loves me enough that he sought me out too.

And maybe I pray that I may see these kids, their parents, and everyone around me as God sees them.

Perhaps we all need to pray that our vision may be changed. God loves us all so much that he was willing to come and be with us, with all our dirt, all our filth, all our failings, and he loved us enough that he served us, healing diseases and doing good in places no one else would go. He loved us enough that he died for us so that we might live with him forever. He loved us enough to seek us out, filthy and stubborn as we are, and to call us his own, his prized possession. And he loves us enough that he still seeks us out even today, in both the nice and the not-so-nice parts of town. What better God and king could we ask for?

I still drive and walk and live here in this neighborhood. I still see the drunk, stubble-faced old men, I still see the drugs, I still see the women selling themselves for money. And yet I'm beginning to learn that while things may look pretty rough, in God's eyes I'm surrounded by diamonds.

Thanksgiving Day
Luke 17:11-19; Psalm 65
by Keith Hewitt

Thanksgiving

I am prejudiced. I may as well put that on the table now, so it's not niggling at the back of your mind as you read the rest of this. Is he, or isn't he? The answer is, I am.

I am prejudiced because I feel that the best way to experience these things is to lie on a furniture pad on a lawn on South 32nd Street, beneath a clear, moonless sky; or to sit by a fire on the Wisconsin shore of Lake Michigan on a black velvet night, with the slow rhythm of the waves matching the rise and fall of your chest.

If you can't do that, at least try to slip away from the streetlights and the traffic lights, and get out somewhere where you can actually see the stars. Let yourself be bathed by the gentle shower of photons from thousands of distant suns, and contemplate the fact that most of that light left its stars before you were born — much of it before your parents or grandparents were born, going back and back, beyond the pyramids. Some of those bundles of energy were just leaving their solar systems when your ancestors were painting animals on cave walls.

And they fall upon you now, exhausted after their long journey, but still bright enough to see.

Look up and know that for every star you see, there are 50 million more that you can't see in our galaxy alone. Leave our galactic neighborhood, and there are 100 billion other galaxies out there — archipelagos of stars, clusters of galaxies strung out across the universe and back toward the beginning of time.

And beneath you? Beneath you is a ball of stone and water, metal and gas that came to be in what some astronomers call the "Goldilocks Zone": that narrow band that loops around our sun, where the temperature is not too hot and not too cold. A ball of star stuff, they tell us, elements expelled from suns whose light has long since faded, elements sent out into the universe to gather again, somewhere, and perhaps relight another solar fire against the darkness or form a planet.

As it slices through this temperate zone of life, there is a wobble to its path, spinning it just enough out of sync to create the precession of seasons, mirroring the cycle of life — birth, growth, aging, dying — year after year, age after age. We mark our lives by the seasons, tick our time off by the whirling of the planet.

Look up at the sky and fall into it, surround yourself in wonder. Chase the light far enough back, and you might find the time when there was nothing… until there was everything. Feel the wind brush your cheek, hear the whirring of the insects, draw breath and hold it, listen for the sound of your own heart beating.

And say thank you. Thank the Lord for this universe of wonder and the gift of abundant life. Thank the Lord for the majesty we take for granted and the glory of creation. Just for a moment, forget all the things that occupy your thoughts, all the worries of the day, and say, "Thank you."

And in the quiet of your heart, in the rustling of the leaves, you just might hear, "You're welcome!"

About the Authors

David O. Bales was a Presbyterian (USA) pastor for 33 years, and is a graduate of the University of Portland (where he was editor of the yearbook) and San Francisco Theological Seminary. In addition to his ministry, he also has taught college: World Religions, Ethics, Biblical Hebrew and Biblical Greek (recently at College of Idaho). He has been a freelance researcher, writer, and editor for Stephen Ministries. His sermons and articles have appeared in *Interpretation, Pulpit Digest, Preaching, Lectionary Homiletics, Emphasis,* and *Preaching the Great Texts*. He wrote a year-long online column: "In The Original: Insights from Greek and Hebrew for the Lectionary Passages." His books include: *Gospel Subplots: Story Sermons of God's Grace*; *Toward Easter and Beyond*; *Scenes of Glory: Subplots of God's Long Story*; and *To the Cross and Beyond: Cycle A Sermons for Lent and Easter*, all available at CSS Publishing Company.

Scott Dalgarno is pastor of Wasatch Presbyterian Church in Salt Lake City, Utah. Born in California, he has previously served four Presbyterian churches in Oregon. He is a graduate of Whitworth University, University of Oregon, and San Francisco Theological Seminary. A poet, his poems have appeared in *The Christian Century, America, The Antioch Review,* and *Yale Review*.

Keith Hewitt is the author of three volumes of *NaTiVity Dramas: Nontraditional Christmas Plays for All Ages* (CSS). He is a local pastor, co-youth leader, an occasional speaker at Christmas events, and former Sunday school teacher at Wilmot United Methodist Church in Wilmot, Wisconsin. He lives in southeastern Wisconsin with his wife, two children, and assorted dogs and cats.

Craig Kelly received his B.A. from the University of Saskatchewan in 2002. He and his wife, Beth, are actively involved in their church, working both in their church's children's ministry as well as working with low-income youth in their neighborhood. Craig enjoys reading, music, hiking, biking, and indulging in old sci-fi movies.

C. David McKirachan is pastor of the Presbyterian Church at Shrewsbury in central New Jersey. He also teaches at Monmouth University. McKirachan is the author of *I Happened Upon a Miracle* and *A Year of Wonder* (Westminster John Knox).

Rick McCracken-Bennett is an Episcopal priest, storyteller, writer, musician, and church planter. He is a member of the Storytellers of Central Ohio and the National Storytelling Network. His doctoral dissertation concerned the use of story to guide congregations into the future that God intends for them. He is the rector of All Saints Episcopal Church in New Albany, Ohio, where a sermon wouldn't be a sermon without a good story.

Stan Purdum, a United Methodist minister, is a freelance writer and editor. His books include *He Walked in Galilee*, about the ministry of Jesus (Abingdon Press, 2005) and *New Mercies I See*, short stories about God's grace (CSS Publishing Company, Inc., 2003), as well as four books about bicycling. He has been published in religious and secular journals, has authored numerous sermons for lectionary volumes and preaching journals, and writes adult Sunday school curriculum. Stan and his wife, Jeanine, live in North Canton, Ohio. They have three grown children.

Frank Ramirez has served as a pastor for nearly 30 years in Church of the Brethren congregations in Los Angeles, California; Elkhart, Indiana; and Everett, Pennsylvania. A graduate of LaVerne College and Bethany Theological Seminary, Ramirez is the author of numerous books, articles, and short stories. His CSS titles include *Breakdown on Bethlehem Street*, *Partners in Healing*, *He Took a Towel*, *The Bee Attitudes*, and three volumes of *Lectionary Worship Aids*.

Argile Smith is Vice President for Advancement at William Carey University in Hattiesburg, Mississippi. He previously served at New Orleans Baptist Theological Seminary (NOBTS) as a preaching professor, chairman of the Division of Pastoral Ministries, and director of the communications center. While at NOTBS, Smith regularly hosted the Gateway to Truth program on the FamilyNet television network. He has also been the pastor of several congregations in Louisiana and Mississippi. Smith's articles have been widely published in church periodicals, and he is the author or editor of four books.

Peter Andrew Smith is an ordained minister in the United Church of Canada, currently serving St. James United Church in Antigonish, Nova Scotia. He is the author of *All Things Are Ready* (CSS), a book of lectionary-based communion prayers. He is also the author of a number of stories and articles, which can be found listed at www.peterandrewsmith.com.

The Rt. Rev. John S. Smylie, Bishop of Wyoming, previously served as the rector of St. Mark's Episcopal Church in Casper, Wyoming, and as the dean of the Cathedral of St. John the Evangelist in Spokane, Washington. He is a published author and storyteller as well as a singer-songwriter. Smylie recently completed *Grace for Today*, a collection of

25 stories that explores how grace, loss, and restoration are part of the same fabric.

John Sumwalt is the pastor of Our Lord's United Methodist Church in New Berlin, Wisconsin, and a noted storyteller. He is the author of nine books, including the acclaimed *Vision Stories* series and *How to Preach the Miracles: Why People Don't Believe Them and What You Can Do About It*. John and his wife Jo Perry-Sumwalt served for three years as the co-editors of *StoryShare*. A graduate of the University of Wisconsin-Madison and the University of Dubuque Theological Seminary (UDTS), Sumwalt received the Herbert Manning Jr. award for parish ministry from UDTS in 1997.

If You Like This Book...

Please go to **www.csspub.com** or 800-241-4056 to order any of the below titles.

Some titles **Stan Purdum** has written and contributed to for CSS Publishing.

New Mercies I See
978-0-7880-1958-6 — printed book $12.95, e-book $9.95

Sermons on the First Readings, Series II, Cycle A
978-0-7880-2451-1 — printed book $37.95, e-book $29.95

Hear My Voice
978-0-7880-2400-9 — printed book $29.95, e-book $19.95

Leading to Easter: Sermon and Worship Resource
978-0-7880-1931-9 — printed book 11.95, e-book $8.95

Worship Resources for Special Sundays
978-0-7880-1974-6 — printed book $12.95, e-book $9.95

Christmas Treasures
978-0-7880-1976-0 — printed book $25.95, e-book $19.95

For other resources authored or contributed to by Stan Purdum, please visit www.csspub.com and type "Purdum" in the Search box option on the left hand side of the page.

Prices are subject to change without notice.

John Smylie contributed to
Sermons on the Gospel Readings, Series III, Cycle B
"We Wish to See Jesus" for Lent/Easter
978-0-7880-2544-0 — printed book $37.95, e-book $29.95

Rick McCracken-Bennett contributed to
Sermons on the Gospel Readings, Series III, Cycle C
"Where Would You Go to Meet Jesus?"
middle third Pentecost
978-0-7880-2621-8 printed book $37.95, e-book $29.95

Keith Hewitt
NaTiVity Dramas
978-0-7880-2483-2 — printed book $12.95, e-book $9.95
NaTiVity Dramas: The Second Season
978-0-7880-2641-6 — printed book $14.95, e-book $9.95
NaTiVity Dramas: The Third Season
978-0-7880-2695-9 — printed book $18.95, e-book $9.95

David O. Bales wrote
Scenes of Glory
978-0-7880-2554-9 — printed book $22.95, e-book $9.95

Sermons on the Second Readings, Series II, Cycle A
"Toward Easter and Beyond" for Lent/Easter
978-0-7880-2452-8 — printed book $37.95, e-book $29.95

For other resources authored or contributed to by David Bales, please visit www.csspub.com and type "Bales" in the Search box option on the left hand side of the page.

Prices are subject to change without notice.

Peter Andrew Smith
All Things Are Ready
978-0-7880-2487-0 printed book $11.95, e-book $8.95

Argile Smith
Walking With God
Proper 23 Through Thanksgiving, First Readings, Cycle A
978-0-7880-2630-0 — printed book $12.95, e-book $9.95

Some books John Sumwalt has written and/or edited for CSS Publishing.
How to Preach the Miracles, Cycle A
978-0-7880-2457-3 — printed book $19.95, e-book $9.95

Life Stories: Study in Christian Decision Making
978-0-7880-0330-1 — printed book $11.95, e-book $8.95

For other resources authored or edited by John Sumwalt, please visit www.csspub.com and type "Sumwalt" in the Search box option on the left hand side of the page.

Frank Ramirez has written and contributed to many different books for CSS Publishing.
Breakdown on Bethlehem Street
978-0-7880-2640-9 — printed book $7.95, e-book $5.95

Come All Ye Faithful
978-0-7880-2485-6 — printed book $8.95, e-book $6.95

Lectionary Worship Aids, Series VII, Cycle C
978-0-7880-2404-7 — printed book $24.95, e-book $19.95

Prices are subject to change without notice.

Gabriel's Horn
978-0-7880-2385-9 — printed book $7.95, e-book $5.95

The Christmas Star
978-0-7880-1915-9 — printed book $9.95, e-book $7.95

For other resources authored or contributed to by Frank Ramirez, please visit www.csspub.com and type "Ramirez" in the Search box option on the left hand side of the page.

Prices are subject to change without notice.

www.ingramcontent.com/pod-product-compliance
Lightning Source LLC
Chambersburg PA
CBHW071713160426
43195CB00012B/1670